BREAK DOWN THE BARRIERS—AND EXCEL

"This book teaches mental toughness to runners who race. Don't let either of the words 'mental' or 'toughness' scare you . . . At its simplest level, mental training means thinking through all that you do and learning why some of it works and some of it doesn't . . . You may not think toughness is a trait of yours. But running toughness isn't the meanness that an NFL linebacker directs against an opponent. Ours is a quiet, long-suffering toughness, directed as much inward as outward. It's less a killer instinct than a survival instinct. Our toughness is made up of equal parts of persistence and experience. We don't so much outrun opponents as outlast and outsmart them, and the toughest opponent of all is the one inside our heads . . . ."

THINK
FAST

JOE HENDERSON, columnist for *Runner's World*, is a best-selling running author. He has written extensively for running magazines, and other publications, since the 1960's.

THINK
FAST

MENTAL TOUGHNESS
TRAINING FOR RUNNERS

Other Books by Joe Henderson

Long, Slow Distance: The Humane Way to Train (1969)
Road Racers and Their Training (1970)
Thoughts on the Run (1970)
Run Gently, Run Long (1974)
The Long Run Solution (1976)
Jog, Run, Race (1977)
Run Farther, Run Faster (1979)
The Running Revolution (1980)
Running, A to Z (1983)
Running Your Best Race (1984)
Running: For Fitness, for Sport, and for Life (1984)
Joe Henderson's Running Handbook (1985)
Total Fitness: Training for Life (1988)

THINK
FAST

MENTAL TOUGHNESS
TRAINING FOR RUNNERS

JOE HENDERSON

A PLUME BOOK

PLUME
Published by the Penguin Group
Penguin Books USA Inc., 375 Hudson Street,
New York, New York 10014, U.S.A.
Penguin Books Ltd, 27 Wrights Lane,
London W8 5TZ, England
Penguin Books Australia Ltd, Ringwood,
Victoria, Australia
Penguin Books Canada Ltd, 2801 John Street,
Markham, Ontario, Canada L3R 1B4
Penguin Books (N.Z.) Ltd, 182-190 Wairau Road,
Auckland 10, New Zealand

Penguin Books Ltd, Registered Offices:
Harmondsworth, Middlesex, England

First published by Plume, an imprint of New American Library,
a division of Penguin Books USA Inc.

First Printing, August, 1991
10 9 8 7 6 5 4 3 2 1

LIBRARY OF CONGRESS CATALOGING IN PUBLICATION DATA:

Henderson, Joe, 1943-
    Think fast : mental toughnes training for runners / Joe Henderson.
        p.   cm.
    ISBN 0-452-26610-6
    1. Running—Psychological aspects. I. Title. II. Title: Mental toughness training for runners.
    GV1061.8.P75H46   1991
    796.42—dc20
                                                                                91-2226
                                                                                CIP

Printed in the United States of America

BOOKS ARE AVAILABLE AT QUANTITY DISCOUNTS WHEN USED TO PROMOTE PRODUCTS OR SERVICES. FOR INFORMATION PLEASE WRITE TO PREMIUM MARKETING DIVISION, PENGUIN BOOKS USA INC., 375 HUDSON STREET, NEW YORK, NEW YORK 10014.

To Barbara, for sharing strength and wisdom.

— CONTENTS —

—FOREWORD—

Are We Tough Enough?

Before writing a book of advice, the author needs to know what his would-be readers might want to know. Before buying such a book, potential readers must know the author's credentials as an advisor. Before the advising begins, let's get acquainted.

I have been running in races since 1958, have been writing about training and racing since 1960, and have been speaking at running seminars since 1970. Almost-daily talks with runners over the years have made me aware of their main concerns. You probably share many of them.

You care little about the news that other, faster runners make. You care very much about how well you, yourself, run. You want to know how you might run better: farther and faster, with better health, more energy, greater enthusiasm. Your concerns are those of a doer, not a viewer. You didn't open this book to find gossip and trivia about big-name athletes. Nor are you a student of psychology, a psychologist who works with runners, or a running coach.

Your concerns are personal. You are a runner, yes, but a special type of runner. You're a "middle-class runner." You have no illusions about making an Olympic team or making a living from the sport, but neither will you settle for minimal running. You don't run as hard or as well as an elite athlete. But neither do you run as cautiously as an exerciser. Long-term, healthy running is one of your goals. Your other goal—short-term improvement of distances and speeds—often conflicts with the first. You won't limit yourself to the few miles a day and few days a week needed for a quick and safe physical tune-up. You want to race, and racing is somewhat risky—both physically and emotionally.

You race mostly on the roads, at distances five kilometers and up. You don't just run in the races; you *race* them. To you, races are athletic contests, not just social events. You race for personal-best times, not just for T-shirts. You have your own goals. They may be to win prizes against other runners, but more likely meeting those goals doesn't require beating anyone. You may be aiming to break a time barrier in the 10K—50 minutes, 45, 40. You may want to finish your first marathon or to qualify for the Boston Marathon.

And now some barrier stands between you and your goals. You aren't tough enough mentally to break down that barrier.

This book teaches mental toughness to runners who race. Don't let either of the words "mental" or "toughness" scare you.

For our purposes, seeking mental help doesn't mean you're a candidate for a psychiatrist's couch—or that you're required to learn the complex and exotic theories and techniques of sports psychology. At its simplest level, mental training means thinking through all that you do and learning why some of it works and some of it doesn't. You can do that without face-to-face professional guidance, just as you can learn to train better physically without hiring a day-to-day coach.

You may not think toughness is a trait of yours. But all runners who race are tough in a special way, and with training can become even tougher. Running toughness isn't the meanness that an NFL linebacker directs against an opponent. Ours is a quiet, long-suffering toughness, directed as much inward as outward. It's less a killer instinct than a survival instinct. Our toughness is made up of equal parts persistence and experience. We don't so much outrun opponents as outlast and outsmart them, and the toughest opponent of all is the one inside our heads.

—Joe Henderson

The Toughness Hall of Fame

Long-distance racing is a sport of speed, to be sure. We admire the runners who finish first. But it is even more a sport of endurance and persistence, of breaking through barriers and overcoming odds. We admire most the runners who won't let difficulties stop them. In a word, they're *tough*.

Pictured alphabetically throughout this book are the author's choices for a "Toughness Hall of Fame." These 25 athletes (by no means a complete list) from events 1500 meters and up have combined the best of two worlds: speed and endurance.

Photographer credits follow the athletes' names. Special thanks to John Hendershott for supplying the photos from *Track & Field News*.

Abebe Bikila *(Track & Field News)*
Ron Clarke *(Track & Field News)*
Derek Clayton (Mark Shearman)
Buddy Edelen *(Track & Field News)*
Jack Foster (Mark Shearman)
Miki Gorman (Jeff Johnson)
Doris Brown Heritage (Jeff Johnson)
Tatyana Kazankina (Mark Shearman)
Kip Keino—with Ron Clarke *(Track & Field News)*
Ingrid Kristiansen *(Track & Field News)*
Billy Mills *(Track & Field News)*
Rosa Mota (Jeff Johnson)
Steve Prefontaine *(Track & Field News)*
Jim Ryun (Jeff Johnson)
Alberto Salazar (Ken Lee)
Joan Benoit Samuelson *(Track & Field News)*
Frank Shorter (Jeff Johnson)
Mary Decker Slaney (Jeff Johnson)
Francie Larrieu Smith (Ken Lee)
Joyce Smith (Ken Lee)
Peter Snell *(Track & Field News)*
Lasse Viren (Mark Shearman)
Grete Waitz (Ken Lee)
Priscilla Welch (Jeff Johnson)
Emil Zatopek *(Track & Field News)*

THINK
FAST

MENTAL TOUGHNESS
TRAINING FOR RUNNERS

—PART I—
THINKING
OF RACING

CHAPTER 1

Define Toughness in Runners' Terms

*Toughness is finding the will and the skill to run outside
your comfort zone.*

—The Urge to Race—

Bob Plunkett, a lapsed racer, now makes a strong and sensible case against the activity he abandoned. Simply, he calls it unhealthy. The runner from Little Rock, Arkansas, says, "I think racing is a threat to most running programs." It was to his. He once spent "three years—and four stress fractures—stepping up to marathon distance." Plunkett reports that "I don't run races any more. I've hung up my racing flats and said good-bye to injuries. I don't get injured now because I run more sanely."

It's hard to argue with him on health grounds. Competition and the training that goes with it make little sense from that standpoint. Racing hurts. It hurts in the doing (from the fatigue of effort), in the days that follow (from overworked muscles now turned stiff), and sometimes even longer (from overuse injuries brought on by exceeding speed and distance limits).

You know these things, yet you keep racing. Even at a time when the total number of runners supposedly is declining, the count of racers has kept growing from year to year since the so-called Running Boom quieted in the early 1980s.

To understand why so many of us are willing to risk our health at the races, we must understand the split personality of running. It is two distinct activities: an exercise or a sport. Exercise is all about staying within safe limits. Sport is all about pushing them. Exercisers train to avoid pain and fatigue, and sacrifice performance in the name of safety. Athletes run to see how much pain and fatigue they can endure before breaking, and by pushing for maximum performance they put their health on the line.

Athletic extremism once dominated the written advice on running. Advice warning us to exercise caution now prevails. Today's writers sound like well-meaning parents who shout, "Be careful! Don't hurt yourself!" These warnings would, of course, rule out racing as too stressful. They would allow runs no longer than three miles or a half-hour, whichever comes first, and none faster than a comfortable pace. You could never run hills or trails: too risky. Running with others more skilled than yourself would be forbidden: they might pull you beyond safe limits.

You can't be too careful, right? Wrong!

You *can* be too careful if it means giving up what makes your running worth doing. Perfect health isn't everything, not if you view running as more than an exercise.

By training as an exerciser would, your running grows safe, cautious, conservative, minimal. Also flat and bland. Something is missing. You long to exceed the safe limits. Don't read this wrong. Easy days are important, even for a racer. They aren't a form of laziness, but an essential form of preparation for harder days to come.

Few of us can afford to be a pure athlete whose days are all hard. Many of our days must mimic those of an exerciser. Without easing off, we would always be too sore and tired to do the running that makes our running worth doing.

Running safely most of the time allows us to hurt a little when the time is right. Racers like to practice moderation in all things, including moderation.

Even Bob Plunkett, the confirmed nonracer from Arkansas, would agree with that last statement. After retiring from competition, he ran across Ireland—and not for his health.

—The Risks of Racing—

Arthur Newton, a legendary ultramarathoner from the years between the World Wars, wrote, "Wild animals, on a whole, are certainly much healthier than the average modern human. They run plenty but rarely for all they are worth. It is only being scared stiff that will make them extend to their utmost." Animals certainly do run fast—but only for short distances, stopping before they exhaust themselves. Apparently, it is unnatural for them to run for long in a state of what we runners call "oxygen debt." Animals don't like to feel exhausted. So any all-out sprints they take are brief.

We operate with similar controls. It isn't natural for us to go very far full-tilt. An Italian physiologist, Rudolfo Margaria, says that the fatigue product lactic acid begins building after about 15 seconds of running in oxygen debt. We can cover about 100 meters in that time.

Primitive man wouldn't run very far with labored breathing, or on heavy, stiff, or sore legs. Primitives took gentle, loping runs, broken by short bursts of speed and by walks or rests.

Running at its purest is identical to that of wild animals and primitive man: running without tiring by combining long, easy, intermittent runs and only brief explosions of speed. But while advocating natural running, it would be wrong to neglect one fact: modern runners are far removed now from our natural state. We were built to

---

You're Tough Enough If. . .

▲ *You know how different sport running is from exercise running.*
▲ *You acknowledge that racing long and fast is an unnatural act.*
▲ *You accept the risks of exceeding safe speed and distance limits.*
▲ *You calculate your risks carefully and ease off between excesses.*
▲ *You risk having your hard work confused with "masochism."*
▲ *You make a habit of hurting yourself to build some immunity to pain.*
▲ *You tolerate a little pain in the race to feel great pride when the race is finished.*
▲ *You expose all of your strengths and weaknesses when you race.*
▲ *You develop "want-power" for tackling the tough work eagerly.*
▲ *You compete with your real foes: the course, the clock, and the conditions.*

---

run away from emergencies, which are largely absent from modern living. But we still come with a reserve of power for dealing with these emergencies.

Our racing is an unnatural act, true. It's also a contrived emergency that satisfies a primitive urge to take risks. Animals in the wilds will run all-out for extended distances if they're starving and running down food, or if they are trying to escape from a bigger animal that's starving and hunting them. Wild animals face one emergency or the other quite often. But humans rarely face life-or-death chases any more. So we have created artificial ones through sports.

Racing is one of those staged risks. A race isn't meant to be a comfortable run but to be a test of the limits, a primitive lesson in survival. No animal appreciates living so much as one who has been to the edge of death. No human appreciates the comforts of civilized living so much as one who has felt most uncomfortable.

Dr. George Sheehan, who writes on both the medicine and philosophy of running, thinks that to take no risks, to court no dangers, or to press no limits is not to experience life fully. "Every sport has certain risks," he says. "Consider mountain climbing, motorcycling, auto racing. Our risks in running are certainly minimal. But they are there." Dr. Sheehan says that, in terms of minor injuries, "running is a relatively hazardous occupation." Still, he recommends taking controlled risks in the form of racing.

He draws support from Dr. Sol Roy Rosenthal, a University of Illinois professor and an authority on risk taking in sports. Dr. Rosenthal thinks that the craving for risk comes with the human mechanism. "This was carefully calculated long ago," he says. "Risk became sport as well as necessity. Natural risks evolved into challenges and physical feats. They helped mold man's code of honor, pride, and loyalty. They also prolonged his youth and prowess. In time, the old stimuli—the old dangers— were forgotten, but not the effects, not the way man felt. He is still happiest when physically threatened."

For Abebe Bikila (Ethiopia), toughness meant launching the African running revolution, running barefoot when he won the 1960 Olympic Marathon, and, shortly after an appendectomy, becoming the first two-time gold medalist in 1964.

But Rosenthal adds, "Let's be sure to understand that I'm not advocating recklessness. There was nothing foolhardy about the risks your ancestors took. They were calculated risks, well calculated."

Much of this book advises you on how to do the calculating.

—The Body-Mind Struggle—

"It's a horrible yet fascinating sight," wrote Sir Arthur Conan Doyle, "this struggle between a set purpose and an utterly exhausted frame. He was practically delirious, staggering along like a man in a dream." In this description of Dorando Pietri's staggering finish at the 1908 Olympic Marathon, the creator of Sherlock Holmes captured the essence of racing. A race puts you into the classic confrontation between a still-willing mind and a weakened body. When you push your limits, this conflict is unavoidable. There comes a point in all distance races when the "set purpose" and the "exhausted frame" do battle, as they did to the extreme in Pietri's case when he finally was helped across the finish line and disqualified after apparently winning the race.

"Physical effort prevails in training," says European sports psychologist Miroslav Vanek, "and psychic effort prevails in competition."

Racing involves the hardest physical work you do, and yet the emotional demands of the race override the physical demands. You experience emotions in a race that aren't part of everyday training. "Jogging through the forest is pleasant," says Kenny Moore, fourth-place marathoner at the 1972 Olympics and now one of this sport's most thoughtful writers, "as is relaxing by the fire with a glass of gentle Bordeaux and discussing one's travels. Racing is another matter. The mind is filled with anguished fearfulness, a panic."

In one of his early articles, describing Frank Shorter's performance at a Japanese marathon, Moore wrote that "Shorter ran 140 miles per week with consummate nonchalance. A 30-mile day did not strain his prodigious physical resources." Yet before the race Shorter said, "The ordeal is between 20 miles and the finish. My only doubt is that my mind is ready to put my body through that. That's why you have to forget your last marathon before you can run another. Your mind can't know what's coming." Moore added that "exploring the forest is easy. Exploring the limits of human performance is excruciating."

Runners who only run at a comfortable pace see only the flat and quiet forest floor. Racers seek to climb peaks of adventure, and in doing so endure valleys of exhaustion.

Racing looks good from a distance. It's exciting to think ahead to it, pleasant to look back at it. But in the immediate preliminaries and the race itself, the reality hits home. By the time you realize how unpleasant it can be, you can't turn back. Quitting in midrace would hurt worse, and longer, than pushing on.

Ron Clarke, the onetime multi-world-record-holder from Australia, writes about his painful confrontations with himself in his book *The Unforgiving Minute*: "In all my races, I feel some degree of pain. This is not remarkable, because any physical activity in which a person extends himself to the limit causes pain. Sometimes it is an agonizing pain which is scarcely tolerable, and when it comes an athlete has to cope with it as best he can—even if it means deluding himself. I remember in my first marathon the only way I could struggle over the last few miles was from lamppost to lamppost, promising myself that each lamppost would be the last." Clarke concludes that "the pain in a race is caused by complete exhaustion. And the more intense it is, the greater the sense of achievement in overcoming it."

In other words, feelings are mixed. Anticipation offsets anxiety before the race, and pride outweighs pain during and after it. Otherwise, racing wouldn't be worth the effort.

—The Sports Psychology Pioneers—

Dr. Bruce Ogilvie and Dr. Thomas Tutko laid much early groundwork in sports psychology and shaped many of the ideas presented in this book. They introduced runners to this subject in the early 1970s during a series of *Runner's World* interviews stretching over several years.

Dr. Ogilvie welcomed the chance to talk not only about his professional work with runners but also his own running hobby. He had been caught up in the first wave of jogomania in the late 1960s, and the running habit had stuck. The conversations drifted back and forth between objective discussions of his work and subjective references to his exercise/recreation. Ogilvie said, "My professional life is my personal life. I'm totally involved with my work." Besides his sports work, he was at the time a professor at San Jose State University—as was Tutko.

His colleague Dr. Tutko added, "I am the original frustrated jock. I would like to play ball the rest of my life. Unfortunately, I have the motivation but not the talent."

Tutko's and Ogilvie's work in sports had already drawn worldwide attention. Their first book, *Problem Athletes and How to Handle Them*, and their articles in popular magazines such as *Psychology Today* were at once revolutionary, valuable, and controversial. On the one hand, radical athletes of that rebellious era charged the psychologists with putting "a dangerous weapon" into the hands of coaches by teaching them how to "manipulate" runners. On the other hand, traditional coaches resisted letting "shrinks" meddle in their dealings with runners.

They persisted in their studies, and eventually won acceptance and respect for their young specialty. They founded the Institute for the Study of Athletic Motivation at San Jose State which tested athletes by the thousands for mental fitness.

The working tool of the Ogilvie-Tutko athlete-testing program was a 190-part questionnaire called the Athletic Motivation Inventory (AMI). The psychologists called it simply "The Instrument." It wasn't a test in the normal way that students think of tests. There were no passing or failing grades, nor any "right" or "wrong" answers (not immediately, anyway, though competition would eventually do its own kind of grading). You simply chose one of three possible answers that best suited your thinking at the moment. "The first natural response that comes to you," the instructions read, "will generally be the best." One example: "I practice alone so I can get more time in—(a) often, (b) sometimes, (c) seldom." Another: "I would like to become a coach—(a) very true, (b) true, (c), uncertain."

The psychologists then fed completed tests into a computer, which instantly digested your data and printed a description of your "athletic personality." The AMI measured 11 qualities that Tutko and Ogilvie had found to be most crucial to athletic success: (1) drive, (2) aggressiveness, (3) determination, (4) guilt-proneness, (5) leadership, (6) self-confidence, (7) emotional control, (8) mental toughness, (9) coachability, (10) conscientiousness, and (11) trust. (See full descriptions of these traits in the Appendix.)

As Ogilvie and Tutko outlined the traits of "championship character," they noted that mental toughness (which they say is present in an athlete who "can bounce back quickly from adversity") is vital to all athletes. None need it more than distance runners, they said. Desirable attributes most closely related to that toughness are: drive ("aspires to accomplish difficult tasks"), determination ("patient and unrelenting in work habits"), self-confidence ("handles unexpected situations well"), and emotional control ("is not easily upset by bad breaks or mistakes").

Ogilvie's and Tutko's computer printout ranked each of these traits, by percentile, against all other athletes tested at their San Jose State Institute. The closer your score came to a perfect 100, the greater your mental strength was in that area. Finally, the computer printout interpreted and analyzed the test scores. It suggested ways to make the best use of your strengths and to deal with your weaknesses.

"The testing," said Ogilvie, "really provides a fundamental basis for a new form of communication." Ideally, armed with this knowledge, coaches could communicate better with runners—and runners with themselves.

Tutko and Ogilvie made no claim that their Athletic Motivation Inventory could predict exactly how far you could go as a runner, and how long it would take you to get there. They weren't in the forecasting business. Nor did they judge you to be "good" or "bad" runners on the basis of the test scores. They simply provided an individualized guide telling you who you are and how you could become all the runner you could be. "The factors which motivate an individual to athletic competition are unique to each participant," Tutko and Ogilvie once wrote. "We believe that improved individual performance will result when each athlete is aware of these psychological drives."

—The Aggressive Distance Runner—

Sports Illustrated writer Joe Jares noted in a report on the work of Tutko and Ogilvie that competitive runners "carry around a load of aggression corked up inside them, whereas football players get rid of it on the field." Aggressive? That seems out of character for runners, who tend to be mild and even meek by outward appearance. "Aggressive" is the right word, however. Dr. Ogilvie said that aggression and introversion are key traits of runners in general and distance runners in particular. "The one trait that distinguishes runners from athletes in other sports is their high level of aggression," said Ogilvie. "Track athletes look to us to be the most aggressive. Only Grand Prix winners [racing car drivers] beat them in terms of aggression, which is interesting. In fact, you can't be a distance runner *without* aggression. You may be a short dashman without it, because the time is so short. But there doesn't seem to be any way you can go those distances without it."

Olgivie quickly explained the special type of aggression present in runners. Partly because of a tendency toward introspection, we turn the aggression on ourselves rather than on others. "A quality that distinguishes distance runners is self-abasement," said Ogilvie. "They're self-punishing sons of bitches. This doesn't seem to be as prevalent in sprinters, and certainly isn't in field-event athletes. Our research supports the fact that nondistance people are more extroverted."

While field-eventers and sprinters may be more outgoing than distance runners, the differences are relative. Ogilvie and Tutko's studies indicate that track and field athletes as a whole show striking levels of introversion when compared with team-sport performers. "Extroverts don't seem to have the same staying power as introverts do," said Dr. Ogilvie. "That's part of the selection that goes on. Tenacity is part of introversion. It is an obsessiveness—a healthy obsessiveness."

This introverted tendency is even more pronounced in women runners than men, Ogilvie noted. "Outstanding women competitors show a greater tendency toward introversion, greater autonomy needs, and a combination of qualities suggesting that they are more creative than their male counterparts." He added that "women competitors are more reserved and cool, more experimental, more independent than males. We attribute this to cultural repression of women. To succeed in *any* field, a woman has to be able to stand up and spit in the eye of those in charge."

In this comment, Dr. Ogilvie identified a trait that distinguishes runners of both sexes: their great need for autonomy. Runners as a group show a strong desire to be their own boss.

The picture starting to emerge of a runner, then, is of a self-battling, inward-looking loner. These qualities serve you well for enduring hard miles.

—The Oddities of Runners—

A net effect of Ogilvie and Tutko's work was to blow away some of the misty romanticism and the nasty rumors that had surrounded athletes. The sports psychologists' research showed, for instance, that the "character-building" benefits of sports are overrated. But they also emphasized that the sports world isn't filled with, in Dr. Ogilvie's words, "overcompensating, psychoneurotic kooks."

Ogilvie was once asked to comment on two apparently opposing views of runners. The first came from Kenny Moore, Olympic marathoner-turned-writer, who had answered the common charge that distance runners are a bit deranged. Read Moore's lines carefully, because his isn't a negative statement: "Good distance runners are crazy, I'm sure—in much the same way that politicians, corporate presidents, and army generals are crazy.

"Their work hints of obsession. Some mild aberration is perhaps necessary to make it to the top in any field, to spur continued effort when the better-adjusted have settled for the comfortable lower rungs."

John Anderson, a former British national track coach, took a different view: "It is a misconception that [runners] are neurotics. They are perhaps the best-balanced group of people in any community—extremely rational, invariably intelligent, and remarkably able to cope with life."

When asked to choose between the two appraisals, Dr. Ogilvie declined. He said there was some truth in both statements and some overstatement. "We find," he said, "that athletes fall in the upper-middle level in terms of emotional stability. They're a little on the high end, though not terribly different from the general population." Ogilvie indicated that the so-called neurotic athletes (the "overcompensatory greats," as he labeled them) are a distinct minority. But the media gives them much more than their share of attention. "The regular guy who does his job and has his ego intact doesn't get his personality examined in the newspapers. So the public gets the wrong idea that the exception is the rule.

Perhaps one factor, more than any other, explains the public's misreading of runners: we appear to suffer almost every day, yet seem to thrive on it. The term "masochistic" is often pinned on us. Are runners masochistic?

According to Dr. Ogilvie, "Masochism is self-destruction. You can't see running in this negative term. Runners are individuals who love to test their body to the fullest. It's really an aesthetic experience for them. These are people who have to live out to the fullest extension of their abilities. Sure, there's punishment and pain in there. But they're not running *for* the pain. There are few feelings in life that lift you as high as when you've done the best you can, really laid it out. But you can't explain those things to people who have never experienced them."

—The Near-Normal Runner—

Runners aren't entirely normal. We weren't stamped from the typical modern mold, and for that we can be thankful.

Normal is fat, not fit. Normal is watching sports, not doing them. Normal is seeing the road through a windshield, not on foot. Normal means average, and average means uninspired to improve. You may have been that way once but you never intend to sink to that level again.

Far from being ashamed of our abnormalities, we runners glory in them—even exaggerate them. But our differences may not be as great as either we or untrained observers think.

Runners appear odd to people who don't run. Some call us "health nuts," while the more refined critics fit the word "obsessive" into their definition. William Stockton

For Ron Clarke (right, from Australia), toughness meant going for the fastest possible time every time he raced. The Australian set more world records (seven in the 5000 and 10,000 meters alone) than anyone in the modern era. For Kip Keino (left, from Kenya), toughness meant proving that African track runners weren't just high-altitude flukes. After winning the 1500 in the thin air of Mexico City's Olympics, Keino won the steeplechase at near-sea-level Munich.

wrote in a *New York Times* fitness column, "To the layman, it seems obvious that runners are different. They pound through the snow, rain, cold and heat—torturing themselves at night and at dawn, dodging traffic and irritable dogs, and measuring their life in miles per week and running shoes per year." Stockton adds, "To the non-psychologist, runners have a personality quirk in their obsessive [there's that word] devotion to the activity and the fervor with which they testify about how it has changed their life." He says that even the sports psychologists differ on just how much runners differ from the "normal" populace.

Dr. William Morgan thinks the differences are slight. The University of Wisconsin psychologist's studies of runners date back to the mid-1970s. "Our work would suggest that in terms of personality structure, the elite distance runner seems to have a personality profile that is similar to the nonrunner," says Dr. Morgan. He concludes that the popular view of runners as odd characters is "just a myth."

We aren't outright deviates, but two other sports psychologists find us straying somewhat from the normal. David Nieman and Darren George of Loma Linda University, both runners themselves, base this conclusion on their extensive research. Nieman and George studied 231 runners—all male, ranging from world-class athletes to 20-mile-a-week exercisers, with an average age of 30. They were compared with 30-year-old men who didn't run.

Both groups filled out the Cattell 16 Personality Factors Questionnaire. The test rated them on a continuum between, for instance, practical and imaginative, or relaxed and tense. The Loma Linda research team found statistically significant differences between runners and nonrunners in nine of the 16 factors. However, the men who run scored much the same as those who aren't active in the very traits often used to explain our oddities: seriousness, conscientiousness, tough-mindedness, and degree of stability.

The runners were somewhat more reserved, dominant, socially reticent, suspicious, shrewd, and experimenting than their sedentary counterparts. Test results gave runners greater departures from norms in intelligence (suggesting that we know what we're doing, and why) and self-sufficiency (as opposed to group-dependence).

The greatest difference appeared on the conventional/unconventional scale, putting runners far to the latter side of it. The practices of the majority don't rule us, which is another way of saying that runners aren't normal.

On that fact, everyone seems to agree. That's how the public sees us, and that's how we want to be seen.

— The Habit of Working —

"Good distance runners are reputed to possess either great resistance or little sensitivity to pain," writes Kenny Moore. "Yet I doubt whether runners as a group are any more brave when it comes to sitting in dentist chairs or receiving tetanus boosters than the general population."

With an anecdote, Moore explains that distance runners aren't insensitive or masochistic brutes, and that running doesn't immunize them to all pain. "One summer, I was included in a group of runners who were invited to participate in a United States Olympic Committee study of high-altitude training and procedures. The price of our three-week vacation in the Rockies was to submit every Friday to a series of tests that measured lactic-acid content of our blood. It seemed strange to our doctors that while we showed no reluctance to run ourselves into unconsciousness at the end of a hard workout (quite easy to do at 7500 feet), the mention of another session with the needles set us all to whining like tormented alley cats. The explanation, of course, is that we were used to *our kind* of pain. Over the years, we had developed a familiarity with our body that let us know how much of the discomfort of extreme fatigue we could stand. Part of the runner's training consists of pushing back the limits of the mind. But the needle pain was relatively new and exposed our 'innate toughness' for what it was: a learned specialty."

Moore's point is that runners are essentially normal individuals—abnormally well trained to run, but still normal—who tolerate specific, minor discomfort in search of major rewards. In the same vein, miler-turned-TV commentator Marty Liquori once said, "There is no satisfaction without first a struggle and deprivation." Runners tolerate the struggle and deprivation while working to find the satisfaction.

Brian Mitchell, author of the sociological/psychological book *Today's Athlete*, writes, "Perhaps one of the biggest mistakes an observer can make is to look upon [running] as a form of self-immolation. It is doubtful whether a wish for pain, or even for discomfort, characterizes the athlete. He does not look upon himself as a victim brought to the altar of the track to be sacrificed, and does not relish the pain that grows from the latter stages of a race. He distinguishes the pleasure in movement from the inevitable pain which has to be endured.

"The athlete will not like this pain. Rather, he will accept it. He knows that if he is to achieve anything competitively, he must take himself through speeds and distances that will be uncomfortable. This he is prepared to do, in training and racing. But it does not constitute 'immolation.' If an athlete wished to cultivate pain, he would buy himself a bed of nails."

Outside observers make the mistake of thinking that runners are immune to pain. They also tend to see runners as possessing iron willpower and self-discipline. Yet "will" is much like pain tolerance. It's a learned specialty, something that comes with training and racing success. You put up with the "discipline" of running so you can sample its rewards.

What outsiders view as willpower and self-discipline might better be described simply as *habit*: the habit of getting up and out on the road or track each day for training, the habit of enduring the discomfort of racing. Ron Clarke, an Australian who once held nearly all of the world track records from 3000 meters upward, remarked that the hardest work in running is "putting your legs in your shorts and taking the first step." Once your willpower, or whatever, gets you through those small moves, habit takes over.

Talk of willpower as "forcing yourself to do what you don't want to do" was notably absent from Bill Bowerman's running formula. Bowerman, perhaps the greatest

American coach ever, schooled Kenny Moore in the ideas that Moore has expressed here. Bowerman said that cultivating a liking for running is essential to establishing a cycle of success. If you like to run, despite its occasional discomforts, you'll keep doing it and will keep getting better at it. The better you get, the more you'll like it, the more you'll want to run, and so on.

"A banker friend of mine told me that he doesn't feel he has 'worked' a day in his life," said Bowerman, "because he enjoys banking so much. A banker must practice his banking virtually 12 months a year. And a runner must do the same with his running. If he doesn't do it and doesn't enjoy it, he's never going to reach the top. Well, he may not reach the top anyway. But if he enjoys his running, he is getting one of the big prizes that comes from this activity."

── CHAPTER 2 ──

Redefine Winning in Personal Terms

Toughness is competing successfully with your toughest opponent: yourself.

─The Lies of Sport─

Two runners with well-known names, one man and one woman, lead their divisions in each big race. We watch them on television one day and read about them in newspapers the next morning as if they were the only people running. We don't begrudge these two athletes their moments of glory. The way the news business operates, the leaders of the pack supply headlines and choice TV footage.

But as runners who have played a small part in hundreds of big road races, and have led none, we also know how important the rest of the story is. It's the story you'll read in a newspaper only in agate type on the back pages, and see on TV only as an oozing, multicolored mass when the cameras briefly shift their focus off the front-runners to take in the crowd behind.

This story really is thousands of individual stories, each one meaning much more to its author than any developments on the road up ahead. Each runner has his or her own job to do.

While handing out awards at one race, the announcer noted that most of the runners hadn't won any prizes they could place on a mantel or nail to a wall. Then he added, "You all are carrying home something of greater value." The announcer asked those who had run their first race to stand, then those who had run farther than ever before, and finally those who had run their fastest time for this distance. More than half of the crowd stood, and the people still seated applauded. "Will those who think they failed or lost today please hold up your hand?" the runners were asked.

You're Tough Enough If...

▲ *You look up to faster runners with admiration and for inspiration.*

▲ *You don't feel intimidated by or envious of the faster runners.*

▲ *You recognize that winning has little to do with who places where.*

▲ *You race with other runners to improve yourself, not to beat them.*

▲ *You realize that no one in the race can beat you except you.*

▲ *You define victory by personal standards that only you can reach.*

▲ *You know that just participating in a race is a small victory.*

▲ *You view not starting or not finishing a race as a major defeat.*

▲ *You know you stand an equal chance of winning or losing any race you start.*

▲ *You profit from your losses by correcting mistakes next time.*

No one did. "This," said the announcer, "is what the running revolution is all about: to participate is to win, to improve yourself is to win bigger, and the only way to lose is to stop trying."

This running revolution is not one of numbers. Sure, we've all heard that 20 or 25 or 30 million Americans run (depending on which poll you believe, and how strictly you define running and runners), and more than a million of them race on the roads. The numbers boom is an effect of the running revolution, not a cause. Before the sport could enjoy its incredible growth spurt, we had to pass through a revolution of *attitudes*. Mainly, "losers" had to decide they could win. They did that by refuting the Three Great Lies of Sport: (1) there is no gain without pain, (2) there is but one winner, and (3) there is no life after racing.

The First Lie claims that a strong mind must beat a reluctant body into shape. The Second Lie implies that only one person in any race escapes being a loser. The Third Lie says that anyone whose painful work isn't paying off with first-place finishes or the reasonable prospect of achieving them should quit running.

If a group of high school or college runners had been asked 10 or 20 years ago, "When do you plan to quit?" most of them would have answered, "As soon as I graduate," or, "As soon as I stop improving." Indeed, many of them secretly hoped for a serious injury that would let them escape sooner, yet with honor. Ask today's runners the same question about when they intend to stop, and most of them will answer without hesitation, "Never!" And they worry that a big injury will end their running forever.

This shift in attitude, from looking for excuses to stop to fearing having to stop, illustrates how dramatically the running revolution has changed our thinking about racing and training. We've come to know that running is too good to hurt all the time; too good to belong only to the people who run fastest; and too good to leave behind when our own racing times stop improving.

For Derek Clayton (Australia), toughness meant training harder than any marathoner before him—up to 200 miles a week—and being first to break the 2:10 and 2:09 barriers. His 2:08:34 mark remained a world best for 12 years.

—The Naming of Winners—

Sports Illustrated magazine occasionally turns its focus away from who's winning what event and turns one of its best writers loose to examine what the winning means, and how it differs from losing. Frank Deford's words on the subject are worth reviewing.

You say winning is overemphasized? Deford disagrees. He claims that modern sports provide *too few* true winners. He writes, "It was decades ago that [pro football coach] Vince Lombardi allegedly said, 'Winning isn't everything. It is the only thing.' Back then, the bluntness of Lombardi's words shocked many Americans. But today, after years of parroting the contention that we place too much emphasis on winning, the bald truth is that victory in America may actually be less important than it ever has been."

We see the clearest proof of that statement in football's college bowl games and during the pro play-off season. Mediocrity is renamed "parity" and rewarded when teams with .500 records advance to postseason play. This is done largely in the name of commerce. More "winners" promote more spectator interest, which in turn generates greater ticket sales.

However, Deford doesn't target money itself as the root of all athletic evil. "What is bad for sports," he says, "is that they have become so *vocational*. That's where the fun has gone out of it." Sports selection resembles job training. Athletes are driven to choose a career early and at the same time to delay their rewards. "No one is ever really allowed to enjoy the experience of being good," writes Deford. "The high school star is judged not for what he does in high school but for where he might be able to play in college. The top college player is never primarily a college player. He is, instead, athletic livestock being fattened up for the pros. The rookie pro does well mainly so that he'll have more leverage when he becomes a free agent. And, of course, the highest goal to which any athlete can aspire is to be a color man on TV."

Deford then notes a paradox: there have never been more opportunities to win on some level, but only the ultimate champions—Super Bowl, World Series, Olympic Games—are judged to be true winners. Or, as Deford puts it, "the athlete must win everything to be anything."

Running is afflicted with some of these symptoms and immune from others. The wrongs need to be cured, and the rights must be protected.

Distance racing grew popular partly because it overthrew the only-one-winner myth. Races wouldn't draw thousands of people if all but one of them thought of themselves as losers. "Everyone can be a winner" was and is one of the great ideas in this sport, and one that separates it from most other sports. Winning is participating and finishing and improving. Every race gives everyone who runs it a chance to win.

Yet we shouldn't forget the value of losing. Winning isn't guaranteed. The risk of losing, even in the personal terms of reducing times and increasing distances, always should hover over us. Otherwise, there would be no spur to train and race better, and victory wouldn't taste as sweet.

At the same time, we shouldn't cheapen awards by making them available automatically to almost everyone. They must be earned. Reserve the material rewards for a few people (say, the gold, silver, and bronze medalists) who race best in a limited number of categories, instead of awarding more prizes in more divisions in the name of equal opportunity. Honoring a select circle of winners doesn't make the rest of us losers, but merely shows that some runners win bigger than others.

Winning isn't everything, but it still is something. When everyone is allowed to "win" or when no one is, winning means nothing.

—The Emphasis on Winning—

Dr. Thomas Tutko, one of the world's foremost sports psychologists, has tested tens of thousands of athletes to find the inner forces that drive them. He is a lecturer to sports audiences, a consultant to teams as high as the professional level, an author of sports books, and a sports participant and fan. These credentials show him to be anything but antisports. And yet Tutko is disturbed by some of the directions sports have taken. He has written in the book *Beyond Winning* that victory in competition is grossly overemphasized at the expense of other, greater values. He called for redefinition of the word "winner." It has to be more than, "Did you finish first or didn't you?"

Says Tutko, "If all you gained was a rinky-dink little medal that collects dust in your room, you've missed the point in athletics. I'd recommend emphasizing those characteristics that everyone can derive from athletics, not just the 'winners.' The emphasis now is on the product and not the process. The product is temporary. The trouble with the product is that it always has to be replaced by another one. After you set a record, you have to run faster next time. That's a hell of a way to live."

What can be gained in addition to medals and records, or beyond them, or instead of them? In Tutko's view, "A race is a miniature of life. There's a start and a finish. You've got to prepare mentally. You've got to go into it with the idea of coming out successfully. It's a struggle, a battle, you and the person ahead of you, or the one behind you, or with yourself. All of these factors are miniatures of life, and adjusting to them is the important factor. It is a model for not quitting in other areas of life."

In Tutko's view, the important lesson for runners to learn is that it's more vital to finish—to run the race as best they can—than to finish first. "Here is the crux of it," says Dr. Tutko. "Life is continually competition, whether you're competing for a job, competing in school, or if you're in the wilderness trying to survive. There's no way you're going to avoid competition, because it is part of life itself. If we emphasize that it is not competition alone but winning that is most important, we've made the burden which is already painful now intolerable. If we say losing is like death, no sane person is going to want to compete. Maybe the best thing athletics can contribute is to teach us to face competition realistically—not to run away from it, or deny it, or shy away from it, but to get in there and compete well. And whatever the outcome, to be able to adjust to it."

—The Leaders and the Followers—

Roger Bannister, as every student of running history knows, was first to break four minutes in the mile. What many people don't remember is who broke it second—and broke Bannister's short-lived world record in the process. That was John Landy of Australia.

The two milers met later in 1954, after setting the record separately that year. It was a classic duel of front-runner versus follower. Landy led most of the way. Then when the Australian heard accelerating footsteps, he cast a panicked glance to his right—the wrong way—and that look cost him the race. Bannister slipped past on the other side and won before Landy could recover.

This is a common tactical error. We lose by looking the wrong way. We check only to see who is beating us instead of noticing that we've already won.

You may have long since accepted the fact that you'll never run as fast or as far as the top finishers. But you're still tempted to look up to them with envy, and to feel like a loser by comparison. For instance, you might place 98th in a road race. You might think, "Ninety-seven people were better today." But that's only one way to look at the results. You've only looked ahead and seen yourself running last of the people within view. If you insist on ranking yourself against other runners, look both ways. Appreciate that some of them will always be faster than you, but also notice that many more are slower.

Count the runners behind you as well as those ahead. Match yourself against all the runners in the field, against those who finished and those who didn't, and against people who never started. First, compare yourself with everyone in this race. The number you're handed at the finish line tells your overall place. It only starts your calculation of rank that accounts for people both in front and in back of you, and for races of different sizes.

Give your place number more meaning by turning it into a percentage ranking. Divide the place by the total number of starters. Nonfinishers are charged with a loss by default. You automatically beat everyone who doesn't make the distance, so you may get to outrun world-class runners. For example, you finish 98th in a field of 609. This ranks you in the top 16 percent, meaning you beat more than four-fifths of the starters. In the next race, you might rank 200th of 2000. You placed lower than last time, but you did better by beating 90 percent of the field.

Next, compare yourself with runners like yourself. In long-distance races, everyone usually starts together, but the results are split into divisions that allow for the inequities of sex and age. Divide your place in the group by its number of starters. If you're old or female, you'll score higher in percentile rank among peers than overall.

Finally, compare yourself with people who dropped out before this race began. If you once ran in high school, think of how many old teammates stopped at graduation. About 90 percent of young runners drop out then. Another 90 percent of the high school survivors drop out in college. So if you still run after leaving school, you're the one original starter in 100 who has kept going.

But wait, the numbers get even better. Do you race now—not just enter races but truly *race* them? If so, you're the one current runner in a thousand who does. If you race marathons, you're one in 10,000.

Look ahead. Don't pretend that you're better than you are. But don't think, either, that you're worse than you are. Ninety-nine-plus percent of runners, past and present, couldn't or wouldn't do what you've done.

—The Competition with Yourself—

The word "compete" holds different meanings for different runners. Competing can mean racing to beat everyone in the field, or the person beside you now, or someone who set a record years ago, or someone who will threaten your mark years from now. Or it can simply mean racing against no one but yourself and the times you once ran.

Distance racing lets you choose whatever type of competitor you want to be. The exact approach you take depends on your ability, but you never need to feel like a loser just because you don't finish first.

Canadian runner Bruce Kidd won against almost everyone he faced while he was still a teenager. Later, when he'd become a well-known writer and political activist, he said, "Sport does not have to be so exclusively competitive that all but the most skilled must be discouraged from participating." Kidd didn't deny the pleasure he'd once taken in beating his elders. But he downplayed the importance of "psyching out" his opponents and focusing a "killer instinct" on them. "Sport doesn't have to be unconditionally aggressive," he said. "Anyone who has been active knows that man-versus-man is but one form of sports conflict. The athlete must compete against himself and the environment, and these common struggles outweigh the interpersonal struggle almost every time."

Kenny Moore, who ran the marathon in 2:11 and placed fourth in the Olympic Games, described his approach to marathon competition: "To be effective over the last six miles, one must harbor some sort of emotional as well as physical reserve. An intensive, highly competitive frame of mind over the early part of the run seems to evaporate after 20 miles." Moore chose to start his marathons in "a low-key, sort of yawning/sleepy state of semiconsciousness. I watched the scenery and the other runners with appreciation rather than any sort of competitive response. I chatted with anyone so inclined."

Only later, after the 20-mile mark, did Moore "try to get enthusiastic about racing. A strong acceleration gave me a lift, and I could usually hold a new rhythm to the finish." He said, "It was more fun to pass people late in the race when it meant something. The last six miles was the stage where I tried honestly to use everything I had left. That, of necessity, hurt."

Note here that Moore talked of making *himself* hurt, not of inflicting pain on someone else. Late in a long race, you may barely notice that anyone else is running. You're fighting a private battle.

Early in his career, Olympic Marathon champion Frank Shorter sometimes intentionally tied for first place with his teammate Jack Bacheler. This outraged some purists, who charged Shorter and Bacheler with working against the purpose of competition. To this, Frank replied, "Maybe in part our tying is an attempt to thumb our nose at the whole idea that the goal is to trample everyone underfoot, to put on your spikes and run over them. It isn't all or nothing with me." He added that "I don't consider coming in second to be losing. It's just not winning. If you're satisfied with what you've done, you haven't lost."

Make no mistake: Shorter competed hard. He didn't win Olympic gold and silver medals without being a competitor. Frank, in common with most distance racers of all abilities and in all events, knew who his main competitor was. He looked at him in the mirror every morning.

—The Quitting of Races—

You're weaned as an athlete on the thought that you should always finish what you start. If you tough out a race, you'll feel better than if you dropped out. That's not always true, of course. Quitting can never be a victory, but it can cut your losses. There is no shame in dropping out to ensure that you can run again another day. Stopping for worsening injury, sudden illness, or impending heat collapse is the only choice that makes any sense.

In the absence of these symptoms, however, there are few terms of surrender that a distance racer will—or should—accept. Enduring to the finish the normal, temporary distress of a race is one way that anyone can win.

Simply finishing is the first level of winning. For many runners, a slow race beats an incomplete one almost every time.

But not everyone agrees with this thinking. Top marathoners run for time and place, and just to finish means little to them. At the 1987 World Championships Marathon in Rome, for instance, 28 percent of the men and 21 percent of the women quit early. Even allowing for humid heat, these figures are way out of line with the average attrition rate of 10 percent for mass marathons. This isn't to suggest that certain individuals didn't have sound reasons for dropping out. But overall statistics indicate that thoughts about seeing international championship marathons through to the end changed in the 1980s.

American marathoners hit their all-time peak at the 1972 Olympics. Not only did Frank Shorter win, but Kenny Moore finished fourth and Jack Bacheler ninth. At Montreal, four years later, Shorter and Don Kardong placed second and fourth. Bill Rodgers ran only 40th, but he still went all the way on a bad day for him. Complete U.S. teams have seldom finished since then. They hit bottom at the 1987 Worlds, when only two of six runners got back to the stadium on foot.

In all, 12 official U.S. teams entered marathons in the 1980s. Twenty of the 62 runners—32 percent—dropped out. Ron Tabb was one of them. In fact, he made a practice of quitting races that weren't going well. Benji Durden, his running mate on two international teams, defends Tabb's strategy: "He had the credo: go for the big

For Buddy Edelen (United States), toughness meant breaking the stereotype that Americans couldn't run fast marathons. A 1963 time of 2:14:28 made him the first U.S. marathoner in more than a half-century to set a world best.

run, and save it for another day if things didn't work out. But he also popped more big races when it wasn't expected than any other American I know." Indeed, Tabb ran a startling 2:09:32 to qualify for the 1983 World Championships. Durden adds that "not everyone believes finish-at-all-costs is the best policy in marathoning."

Dropping out when running a bad race isn't wrong. It's just different from the thinking that some of us take to our races. Top marathoners are different from the rest of us, and not only because they run faster. They also don't run as long. The distance still measures 26.2 miles. But it seems shorter and less imposing to the elite than to us, because they do more training and take less time to run the race.

At the highest levels, the marathon is a true race. People up front don't need to prove they can go the distance. Instead, they go for victories measured by time and place, and abandon lost causes.

But at the lower levels, where most of us live, to finish is to win. Quitters can't win, and winners can't quit.

—The Reward of Finishing—

That great cliche of running, "Everyone is a winner," is flawed. Everyone also faces the prospect of *losing* to the toughest of opponents.

We race together but compete alone against the elements: distance and time, surface and terrain, temperature and wind. Every runner stands a chance of losing against these elements, particularly when the distance exaggerates their effects as it does in the marathon.

Mark Nenow, the world's fastest 10-K road racer, was very slow to try his first marathon. "The marathon is a big, smiling face with a hand stretched out to you," he once said. "But I have this feeling the marathon is a devil in disguise. There's an element of destruction in the marathon." It can be destructive to body and spirit, and therein lies its attraction. The runner challenges the devil, that two-headed demon of injury and exhaustion.

If success were guaranteed, the race wouldn't be worth running. And if failure were inevitable, the risks wouldn't be worth taking.

Marathoners don't live as dangerously as football or hockey players, skydivers or boxers. Running-induced ailments rarely are severe or permanent. But marathoners willingly, even eagerly, gamble with their health.

This isn't to say that they can afford to be foolhardy. Without some easier training, they would be too sore and tired to race. But without racing, they wouldn't know their potential.

The marathon takes more runners farther into areas normally left unexplored than any other race. That's the main reason most people run this distance. They don't come to marathons to win prize money or divisional awards, or for the chance to start with the stars. They come for the chance to take chances, to make some unknowns known, to win without having to finish first.

Among running events, the marathon beats all others as a natural attraction because it is more than just a race. The 10-K is a race, a speed test. But for most runners, the marathon is a *survival* test where native speed and skill count for less than careful preparation and dogged persistence. Getting to and through a marathon is an experience never to be forgotten.

Spectators whose only view of the marathon comes from the last mile may not see what runners see in this event. Casual observers might call it a depressing sight. Men and women teeter on the brink of exhaustion. They run stiff-legged, as if feet would break and muscles would tear if they took a normal stride. Some of them list out of balance to protect an injury or cramp. Most of them are oblivious to all sights and sounds, so focused are they on the goal now only minutes away.

The picture will soon change. Runners two hours and 2000 places behind the leaders will dance across the finish line as best they can on sore and tired legs. Some of these people will shout for joy, while others will cry for the same reason.

There are no easy marathons, and maybe that's the point of running them. While everyone who enters has a chance to win against the elements, victories must be earned. Those that cost the most give the most in return.

A nonrunner recalls the aftermath of his wife's first marathon. He was alarmed at the sight of her at the finish line. She seemed to have aged 20 years in four hours, and now had trouble using the legs that had carried her all this way. "She was so stiff, she could hardly move," says the husband. "I might have been tempted to call an ambulance to transport her to a hospital—except all the time she kept moaning about what a fantastic experience it was, and how she wanted to do it again next year."

—The Definitions of Victory—

"Winners never quit, and quitters never win." That slogan graces thousands of locker-room walls and supports many a coach's pep talks. And it's true, but not in the way that your high school coach meant.

You wouldn't think of quitting while you're winning. So the way to keep from ever quitting is to define defeat and victory in ways that can make us all winners. Some of those definitions:

- *Winning is realizing that you already have won something just by being in the race.* You may not finish ahead of many other people but you have already beaten a much bigger pack that didn't start.

  Losing is not starting, but being content to talk about what might be or what might have been... if.

- *Winning is going the distance.* Speed is a gift, but endurance and persistence are learned. Finishing is a victory of the will you've trained to be strong.

  Losing is dropping out for no other reason than a weak will. Giving in to moderate inconvenience or mild discomfort is defeat.

- *Winning is measuring yourself against yourself.* It is, first, learning to take pride in your improvements. Later it is taking pleasure in more subtle measures of victory that have little to do with time or place.

  Losing is matching yourself against everyone else who runs. This is self-defeating, because few people ever win this way—and those who do don't stay on top for long.

- *Winning is recognizing your relative ability.* You look up to the people ahead of you for advice and inspiration, but without feeling envious or inferior to them.

  Losing is being intimidated by runners ahead of you or superior to everyone who trails you.

- *Winning is working with other runners* so all of your results are better than any of you could have achieved alone.

  Losing is knocking someone else down, figuratively or literally, so you can look taller. It is interfering in any way, physically or psychologically, with another runner's progress.

- *Winning is accepting the results* as they come, knowing that every race won't be a good one. The bad days provide contrasts to help you appreciate the good ones.

  Losing is choosing to ignore your losses or to make excuses for them.

- *Winning is learning from your bad races.* They often teach better than the good ones, because they force you to look for relief.

  Losing is refusing to accept failure as a teacher or to examine the reasons for failing.

- *Winning is standing on the shoulders of giants.* It is absorbing the written and spoken lessons of people who have run before, instead of using up an entire career resolving by trial and error the puzzles that already have been solved.

  Losing is keeping secret the solutions you've found to training and racing puzzles.

- *Winning is continuing to stay fit* after fate has decreed that you are past your prime and never again will break a personal record. It is going on when you have nothing left to prove at the races.

  Losing is setting goals you either can't reach or can touch too easily. Either way, goals become stopping places. If you don't reach them, you stop from frustration. If you reach them without stretching, they stop you short of your potential.

- *Winning is knowing you are only as good as your last race.* The good effects and feelings don't store well, so you have to renew them regularly. Modest fresh efforts are more rewarding than stale memories of your spectacular races from the past.

  Losing is living in the past. It is trying to get your thrills by reliving old glories instead of finding out exactly where you stand now.

Losing has no future, but winning lasts. Losers quit, but winners survive. And in the long run, a survivor is the best you can be.

Youth fades, speed declines, medals tarnish. The only thing that lasts is lasting.

—— CHAPTER 3 ——

Make Friends with Your Competitors

Toughness is teaming up to accomplish more together than you could do alone.

—The Ties that Bind—

Frank Shorter sat down to dinner in 1971 soon after he'd become a marathoner that day at the National Championship race in Eugene, Oregon. He didn't eat anything. He couldn't: his first marathon had so upset him that he turned green at the sight of food. Seeing Shorter this way demonstrated that faster and slower runners are really only divided by speed. We're much more alike than different. The stars get sick, too. They get hurt. They get tired and bored and worried. They need help from their friends.

Seventeen years passed between witnessing that incident and another involving Shorter. The second one was another reminder that, appearances to the contrary, Frank is still one of us. He was in Charleston, West Virginia, for the 15-mile Distance Run. While there, he attended a stand-up buffet dinner at a country club. Frank exchanged small talk with the sponsors and officials during the cocktail hour. But when it came time to eat, they left him to find their friends. The most famous guest took his meal alone and looked lonely doing it.

Shorter is, in a way, a victim of his fame. As Olympic Marathon champion, NBC-TV track analyst, and spiritual leader of the U.S. Running Boom, he's held in greater awe than ever. His manner makes him appear unapproachable. His prep school and Ivy League training combine with his natural reserve to give the impression that he is cool and aloof.

Frank is treated as royalty, to be admired only from a distance. Runners still are shy about walking up to him and talking about what they have in common. Shorter knows this. He now tries to put people at ease, and as he does a friendly side of him shines through the regal bearing.

You're Tough Enough If. . .

▲ *You make friends with those who understand you best: fellow racers.*
▲ *You receive support from and give it to your best running friends.*
▲ *You team up with a small group with similar interests and abilities.*
▲ *You take your longest and fastest runs of the week with the group.*
▲ *You join a club and take the responsibility of racing as a team.*
▲ *You cooperate with other runners to compete against common foes.*
▲ *You linger after races to share experiences and expertise.*
▲ *You seek help from experts while remaining your own boss.*
▲ *You enlist a coach or an advisor to help with your running problems.*
▲ *You volunteer as a coach or an advisor to help runners in need.*

One by one, runners work up the nerve to approach him. He talks with one about their children (he has six). He tells another runner about returning to his early home of Ward Hollow, West Virginia, where Frank's father had worked as a coal-mine doctor. He talks with a reporter about some of his teammates from the 1972 Olympic Games and what they're doing now. Most are still active in the sport. "We had something then that's missing now," said Shorter. "We trained together. We helped each other. We were friends."

Shorter had intentionally tied for first place with Jack Bacheler in track races as far back as 1970, when they started training together in Florida. Shorter and Kenny Moore had shared first place in the 1972 Olympic Marathon Trial. Shorter, Bacheler, and Jeff Galloway had trained as a team in the Colorado mountains for the Munich Games. Shorter had agreed to share the pace in some of Steve Prefontaine's record attempts.

"You don't see that any more," Frank said. "Maybe the Mormons in Utah [Olympians Ed Eyestone, Henry Marsh, and Doug Padilla] do it to a degree. But otherwise, it's basically every man for himself."

A reporter asked Shorter to assess his role in leading running to where it is now. "I understand my part in all of it," said Frank, "and I respect that I have an image. But what's important to me is that I don't try to be someone I'm not." He is not untouchable. "I want those around me who matter—my family and a few close friends—to appreciate me for who I am. The recognition is nice, but that's not why I do what I do." He does it for most of the reasons we all do.

—The Aloneness and the Togetherness—

Running offers both aloneness and togetherness, in whatever blend you choose. Running time can either be your time to think or your time to talk. Contemplation and conversation can, at different times, each play a valuable role in your running.

For Jack Foster (number 50, from New Zealand), toughness meant competing on even terms with the youngsters after he'd turned 40. He placed second in the 1974 Commonwealth Games Marathon with 2:11:19, a world record for masters that stood for 16 years.

They both do for Dr. George Sheehan. The *Runner's World* columnist thinks up his writing themes on the run. "I take the raw material out on the road with me, with the hope that during the run the one sentence that will set up the entire organization of the column will somehow come to me. More often than not, it does. But I can't force it. I have to wait for it to come."

Other voices would block those thoughts. Yet Dr. Sheehan doesn't always run to think. Sometimes he welcomes talk. "Running frees me from the monosyllabic inanities of my usual tongue-tied state. It liberates me from the polysyllabic jargon of my profession. It removes me from the kind of talk that aims at concealing rather than revealing what is in my heart." Sheehan adds that "for me, no time passes faster than when running with a companion. An hour of conversation on the run is one of the quickest and most satisfying hours ever spent."

You might have started running alone because you had no choice and now continue that way most of the time because you've learned to enjoy being by yourself. Likewise, you might start teaming up occasionally for practical reasons and keep rejoining the group for social ones.

The practical reason for teamwork is mutual support. You can train farther and faster as a team or group than you would alone. Just as running by yourself opens up time you might otherwise never take to think, training with partners gives you the chance you might not otherwise take to talk. Running long distances together encourages conversation, just as running alone leads naturally to contemplation. Perhaps the rhythm of striding jars loose ideas that otherwise might be held inside. Maybe dressing the same way symbolically strips us of the roles we carry the rest of the day and frees us from the verbal posturing we do then. More likely, the talk flows freely because people who enjoy each other's company are sharing a common interest and effort. The run gives us uninterrupted time to converse. Training with a partner or small group for long periods of time, with no other entertainment at hand, breaks down barriers to communication.

Longtime runners say only half-jokingly that running develops one set of muscles more than any other: those that operate the mouth. Those same muscles also are slowest to tire.

A runner who prefers aloneness can easily find it. On the other hand, one who wants running to be a sociable activity can plug into a support system. Here are a few hints for forming a training group and keeping it harmonious:

1. *Make it rewarding.* Offer something in the group effort (besides the talk) that a runner can't or won't find alone. For instance, a weekly extralong training session or speed work.
2. *Keep it small.* Two is the minimum number, of course, but two leaves no spares if someone is absent. More than five makes the group unwieldy and impersonal. Three or four is the ideal group size.
3. *Think and act alike.* Form a group with similar abilities and ambitions. Nothing splits you up faster than disagreements over paces and distances.
4. *Be regular.* Have a standard, agreed-upon meeting place and time so no one needs to make special scheduling arrangements each time.

5. *Stay together.* Train at the pace of the slowest member of the group so you can all join in the conversation and receive the mutual support.

—The Work of Teams—

On the face of it, running isn't much of a team sport even for school teams. Only a common uniform links the members of a track team. Milers and shot putters are as unrelated to one another as swimmers are to football players. Mixing their results in the scoring says little about the team's running talent. Even the distance runners separate into different events on the track. They really only team up for relays, where the four runners still compete separately—linked only by a baton. In cross-country, everyone runs the same race at the same time, then the runners pool their places for a team score. But even here, an individual can succeed even while the team fails.

Team scores mean little in running. But team *spirit* does mean a great deal. This spirit keeps members training and pulls them through rough patches in races where they might stop if teammates weren't counting on them.

Road racing traditionally has appealed to older runners, unaffiliated with schools or clubs. The team spirit was slow to take hold in road racing, but a strong trend toward teamwork finally appeared in the 1980s.

Runners have traditionally treated road races as both social and athletic events. We go to races to be with other runners—to see old friends and to make new ones. But the socializing gets harder to do as events grow. The more people they draw, the less personal they become. Partly in reaction to the lost-in-the-crowd feeling of mass races, runners have regrouped in more sociable ways.

Teamwork appears in what seems to be the loneliest of pursuits, ultramarathoning. The ultrarunners are what marathoners were a generation ago and race walkers still are: a fringe group banded together for mutual support from the only people who understand what they do and why.

The caring extends to the helpers. At a time when standard events have cracked down on all forms of outside help (such as self-appointed pacesetters), the ultras encourage it. For instance, runners in the Western States 100-Mile Race recruit their own pacers to brighten the late miles.

Teamwork at the more standard distance races now takes more forms than ever before. Older road runners share the excitement, once available mainly to school track and cross-country teams, of being part of efforts bigger than their own.

The Trevira company sponsors a popular race for male/female teams, a 10-miler in New York City. The Foot Locker chain promotes a national series of events for couples of various combinations. The Alamo car rental agency conducts Alumni Runs for ex-college teams.

Businesses put together teams for the well-attended Manufacturers Hanover series of road races. *Runner's World* launched the popular Corporate Cup competitions on the track.

Internationally, the sport's governing body now promotes the World Challenge—a relay of marathon length. In the U.S., road relays boomed in popularity during the 1980s. Hundreds of teams (of 12 runners each) enter the 191-mile Hood to Coast Relay in Oregon each summer. Some runners who've never teamed up before now worry about carrying their share of the load in this event. "In other races," said one woman running on her first team, "you only disappoint yourself by not doing well. Here, you let down 10 other people." After the race, however, this runner called Hood to Coast her best running experience to date. She said, "I went farther and faster than I ever could have gone without team support."

This story illustrates the two sides of teamwork. Running for a team adds worry about letting down your teammates, but also multiplies the joy of success. The worry makes you work harder. And by giving more of yourself to the team, you get more from and for yourself in return.

Extra effort comes more easily when someone else is counting on you. Success tastes extra sweet when you can share it with teammates.

— The Job of Coaching —

"Being in politics is like being a coach," said onetime senator, onetime presidential candidate, and sometime poet Eugene McCarthy. "You have to be smart enough to know the game, and dumb enough to think it's important." McCarthy made this statement in jest. He felt politics was important enough to invest most of his life in the "game." And he greatly admires coaches who do the same in theirs.

His analogy is a good one. Coaches are a lot like politicians. The coach's decisions affect the lives (athletic ones, at least) of the people who place trust in them. Coaches, like politicians, must know their job, and their effectiveness lies largely in their ability to communicate that knowledge. The best coaches, like the most effective political figures, are those who possess technical skill combined with large doses of persuasive power. The latter trait is put to a stern test when a coach deals with a distance runner.

Sports psychologists Thomas Tutko and Bruce Ogilvie have studied successful distance runners and found them to be self-motivated loners by nature. They also have questioned coaches. The successful coaches, say Ogilvie and Tutko, are "very high in leadership qualities. . . dominant, take-charge types of persons who would actively seek roles of leadership."

You can see the potential for conflict when these two personality types meet. "In terms of our measurements," says Dr. Ogilvie, "runners turn out to be far more autonomous than athletes in other sports. They need independence. They don't brook too much interference or bow readily to authority." He adds that "there has to be a point where a really gifted person turns away from the coach." At that point, the coach who seeks tight control over athletes "feels rejected." But Ogilvie notes that such partings are "the nature of excellence" in this sport.

Distance runners aren't football players. Runners are built along smaller and skinnier lines, of course, but differences in appearance aren't nearly so great as those of attitude. Runners think differently—in the independent, introspective manner that suits our solo activity. And most of all, we compete differently—as individuals and not as teams.

A football player can't play without a team surrounding him. And a football team can't bring order out of chaos without a coach to lead it.

Football's values and running's values differ. Football demands the surrendering of individuality for the good of a smoothly functioning team unit. A football coach can't have his centers, backs, and ends all planning their own plays and executing them on their own.

Runners, however, can perform without help either from a team or from a coach. This isn't to say they'll do their *best* running without team support and coaching counsel. But runners can and do run on their own.

Maximum individual development is the runner's number-one concern. The coach's main job should be to nourish this goal. Recognizing this basic fact of the coach/runner relationship goes a long way toward solving any problems that might come up between the two. Successful coaches see that the independent streak in distance runners isn't to be feared or fought, but accepted and directed.

A good coach teaches runners to coach themselves. Lionel Pugh, a Canadian national coach, says, "I believe a coach's role, like a parent's, should be to kick the fledgling out of the nest as soon as possible. A coach should never be a crutch." Once runners learn to move under their own power, they no longer need to be driven. They don't need a Xeroxed schedule handed out every Monday, to be followed precisely. But they never outgrow their need for guidance and encouragement.

All runners, regardless of their stage of development, can use an advisor to help them past the rough spots. They'll always be a demand for this type of coach.

—The Coach as Advisor—

The training methods of successful running coaches vary to the extreme. So do their coaching approaches. But these coaches share one common trait: confidence in themselves and their methods, both of which they pass on to their runners.

While writing about Arthur Lydiard, a dynamic coach from New Zealand, running writer A. M. LaSorsa comments, "He reveals almost classically the sine qua non of nearly all such individuals: an unswerving, unquestioned, indomitable faith in himself and belief that he is right. It is also the secret of these coaches' success, because this profound faith is transmitted to and acquired by their followers. As long as he and his athletes have this faith in their method of training, the actual method is of little real significance. Hence, coaches with widely differing approaches to training have all produced champions."

Lydiard, perhaps the greatest coach since World War II, hasn't done much coaching—in the sense of working day to day with individual athletes—since the 1960s. In that decade, his runners from New Zealand won five Olympic medals—four of them gold. In his own words, Lydiard now "advises athletes and coaches coaches." He roams the world as a lecturer.

"For a long time," he says, "I have not personally controlled the workouts of my pupils but have acted more the role of an advisor. They have followed my instructions independently. Frankly, once these runners have absorbed the elements of my system, and gained the maturity to understand them and their own reactions to them, they haven't needed my constant presence."

He now urges runners who attend his lectures to hold their coaches accountable. "If the coach says, 'Okay, go out and run 20 times 400 meters,' you say, 'Coach, why am I doing this? What physiological effects is this going to have on me?' If that coach can't tell you, then you go and get another coach, because this one is going to hurt you. It's your career."

Lydiard tells coaches to examine themselves and their methods. "The days of the sarcastic type of coach who spurs his pupils on with sneers and jibes, designed to whip them to greater effort, are gone. It is the wrong kind of mental stimulus in the modern world. Practical psychology gets the results twice as easily and usually much more effectively. The results also are generally more lasting."

He advises coaches to praise freely. "From the beginning, when you start getting runners fit and set them to training assiduously, let them know when you consider they have done well. Give them full credit for what they put into the work, and they will respond by putting more in. A pat on the back works much better than a kick in the pants."

Lydiard devised a physical training scheme that has been copied successfully the world over. It works even when he has nothing directly to do with its application.

But when asked about his training methods, he doesn't immediately launch into descriptions of 100-mile weeks, hill training, and track work. He tells coaches that "coaching distance runners is like assembling a jigsaw. All coaches know the different methods of training. They all have the parts of the puzzle, but they don't know how to put them together correctly."

He instructs coaches to "know your job, and make sure your athlete *knows* you know it. Then you have established a mutual understanding that is worth more than a book of high-flown technical theory.

"Coaching is more than a science. It is also an art."

—The Shortage of Coaches—

Jumbo Elliott is dead, and Bill Bowerman has trained his last runner. We may never again see anyone coach so well for so long. Elliott coached at Villanova University for about 30 years. He never went without world- and nationally ranked runners in all that time. They ranged from Olympic 1500 winner Ron Delany in the 1950s to 1983 World champion 5000 man Eamonn Coghlan. Bowerman always produced top

For Miki Gorman (right, from the United States), toughness meant enduring the war in Japan, then emigrating to the U.S. and starting to run as an adult. She won the 1976 New York City and 1977 Boston marathons after turning 40.

milers and steeplechasers during his decades at the University of Oregon. His coaching ended in 1988 with the retirement of steepler Henry Marsh.

Coaching dynasties such as Elliott's and Bowerman's aren't likely to develop again. Coaches who work their magic on so many athletes for so many years are an endangered breed. We still have Brooks Johnson at Stanford, Sam Bell at Indiana, and Bill Dellinger at Oregon. Four of Johnson's present or past distance runners competed in the Seoul Olympics. Four of Bell's made World and Olympic teams in 1987-88, as did five of Dellinger's in 1983-84.

But these are minidynasties compared to those of Elliott and Bowerman. Today's coaching climate works against any repeat of their long-term success. This is a tough time to be a coach. One coach calls it a time of "crisis" in his profession.

Skip Stolley has coached running at the high school, college, and club levels. "A scarcity of experienced, skilled coaches is affecting every level of our sport today," he writes. Stolley notes that "at the high school level, participation in track and field has been on the decline throughout the 1980s." Combining this fact with widespread cutbacks in sports and physical education programs, the result is "a vast reduction in P.E./coaching positions across the country."

Budget cuts are also eroding the college sport. "According to the NCAA," writes Stolley, "29 member institutions have dropped their men's track and field programs [along with many women's teams] between 1982 and '88. These included Northwestern, Oregon State, and San Jose State in 1988 alone."

Clubs also offer little support to coaches, says Stolley. "The national club system of athlete development peaked before the 1984 Olympic Games, then collapsed when athletic shoe and apparel companies slashed their sponsorship programs. Fewer funded clubs has resulted in fewer paid coaching positions."

The job market for professional coaches seeking a team to coach is shrinking. But that's only one type of coaching, the traditional type.

Opportunities have never been greater for coaches who don't require a stable of athletes or a regular paycheck. Informal coaching offers unlimited prospects.

Every runner needs a coach. You never stop needing one, no matter how long you run or how wise you think you are. Handling your own running all alone is like acting as your own lawyer or doctor. You're too close to the case to see obvious solutions.

You don't need a babysitter-coach to plan, order, and watch every move. You need a friend-coach to call upon for advice and support.

Every experienced runner is capable of coaching someone else. As the number of veteran runners grows, so does the pool of coaches.

Fred Wilt served as an early model for this type of coach. He later coached formally at Purdue University, but in the 1960s he worked as an FBI agent in Indiana and coached a few runners by mail.

Buddy Edelen lived in England then. Each week, he sent his diaries to Wilt for comment. With that help, Edelen ran a world marathon best of 2:14:28. No other American man has set a recognized mark between 1909 and now.

More recently, long-distance coaching has worked well for other teams of two: Bill Bowerman in Oregon and four-time Olympian Henry Marsh in Utah; Bob Sevene and Joan Benoit on opposite coasts during the gold medalist's 1984 Olympic Marathon training; John Dixon in New Zealand and marathoner Nancy Ditz in the U.S. before she made the 1988 team; Jack Daniels in New York and Ken Martin in New Mexico, Kim Jones in Washington and Benji Durden in Colorado before Martin and Jones each placed second at the 1989 New York City Marathon.

Any smart runner can be this type of coach, and any runner with a phone, a computer modem, a fax machine, or a mailbox can have one.

—The Competitor as Companion—

To Dr. George Sheehan, this was competition at its best. He was running the last mile of a cross-country race when he heard someone coming up from behind. As the younger man pulled alongside and then ahead, Dr. Sheehan called, "Way to go. You're looking great." George didn't surrender meekly but recalls chasing the man as best he could. "Until he challenged me, I had been running to survive, thinking I was doing the best I could. Now I discovered reserves I had not suspected were there. I finished with my best time of the year."

Sheehan says such encounters are "the rule rather than a rarity in running. They embody the essence of the running experience. Nevertheless, the younger man found my encouragement almost incomprehensible. The idea that an opponent would urge you to beat him seemed an impossibility. He became so psyched up, he said, that he ran better than he had thought possible."

This is the best type of competition because you don't have to push anyone down to stand tall. You draw strength from other runners without draining any of theirs.

Dr. Sheehan outlines a racer's creed that encompasses this view of competition: "I am in control of what I do. In the race, my performance is my concern—not yours. In fact, the better you do, the better I will do as well." He calls this "the true nature of competition. The Latin root of the word is *petere*—to go out, to head for, to seek. The *com* is doing it together, in common, in unity, in harmony. Competition is simply each of us seeking our absolute best with the help of each other. What we do magnifies and inspires each of us." In this setting, Sheehan would find it "unthinkable to cheat anyone else or to be diminished by the performance of another."

In other words, no one can beat you but you. This means you don't have to look at other racers as "the enemy." They are there to make you run harder, longer, faster than you could go alone.

You still try to beat them to the finish line, of course. But you know you're only using them to help beat the only competitor who ultimately counts: yourself.

You need to feel none of the hatred that some athletes in other sports must work up against their opponents. You feel no need to use physical or psychological trickery on them.

Your only goal is to get from the start to the finish as quickly as possible. Your sole "tactic" is to take the fastest path.

You're racing together—helping, not opposing, each other. This is the ideal way of looking at competition, anyway.

The reality isn't quite this pure. But don't worry. Sainthood isn't a requirement for entering races. You don't need to love all fellow racers as brothers and sisters. You don't need to abandon all aggressive urges and stop trying to beat people.

You're only required to follow the long-standing custom in distance racing of treating other runners with the same respect that you yourself expect to be treated. Mind your manners, if for no other reason than self-interest. Interfering with anyone else's race would only slow your own.

—The Need to Talk—

Talking among runners peaks after a race. No sooner does the running end than the instant replaying begins.

We talk before races, too, because runners seldom see one another as the enemy. Our enemies are distance and time, the course and the weather conditions, and we face them together.

But before the race, the talk is distracted and restrained. We don't talk much about our common enemies for fear of making them grow more frightening.

During the race runners more often cooperate than compete. We draw strength from the people around us, but the help is mostly nonverbal. Conversation interferes with concentration.

After the race, the real talking begins. The amount varies in direct proportion to the distance covered. The farther we run, the more we're compelled to talk about it afterward.

Leonard Schecter once remarked in *Look* magazine that "people who live with pain, like boxers and long-distance runners, show very little aggression outside the sports arena."

After long races, physical lows and emotional highs occur simultaneously. Runners who've gone through the same discomfort now wallow together in the relief that follows.

As we talk, we rerun each detail of the race, caressing and magnifying it with each telling. The miles grow longer, the hills steeper, the wind stronger, the temperature hotter.

The talk is as much a part of the race as are training for it and pushing through it. Sharing experiences gives the race a final stamp of meaning.

Perhaps the best description of this reaction comes from Kenny Moore. Before he finished fourth in the Olympic Marathon, before he became even better known for his writing in *Sports Illustrated*, Moore wrote an article for his college alumni magazine. It tells why runners talk so much after our races. "Human beings are reluctant to accept meaningless suffering," wrote Moore, "just as families of dead soldiers refuse to believe such sacrifice could be in vain. The pain in a marathon's closing stages can be so great as to *force* meaning upon the run. Runners submit to the ordeal not in spite of the pain but because of it. Competitive urges can carry you 10 or 15 miles. But then the distance and discomfort already endured scream that this must not be for nothing. So you go on."

Moore observed that, after the race, runners "hang stiffly to one another, too exhausted to untie their shoes. And they jabber uncontrollably. The pain has made everything suffered so extraordinarily important that it *has* to be expressed. The cramp which seized your left leg coming off the hills at 20 miles must be described in loving, urgent detail—if only to the wall because nobody listens. Later, when you recover, you remember your babbling and the others', and in an embarrassed sort of recognition you understand you shared something."

It's the same everywhere, for everyone who runs long distances. The postrace scene is part postbattle celebration at having survived, part family picnic, part happy hour at the corner bar.

Thirsty runners are known to drink lots of beer at such parties. But alcohol isn't an essential fuel or even a necessary one. We're drunk on the pain and fatigue we've just felt, on relief that it is over, and on pride that we've endured it. And we must talk about it.

Listen again to Kenny Moore: "Perhaps when one stops, when one comes to accept that this is merely the way pain works on the mind, that there is no inherent meaning in repeating this sort of suffering, one will have died a little. The enduring satisfaction of distance running is not in setting records that will invariably be broken, not in knowing that you were best (read: 'luckiest') on a given day. It lies in knowing that you have learned how to be brave and to do something better than you first thought you could, and perhaps in knowing that you amazed a few people along the way."

If we race to show ourselves we can be brave, we talk long afterward to express the amazement.

For Doris Brown Heritage (United States), toughness meant becoming a distance runner long before women ran distances in the U.S. This most successful cross-country runner, female or male, in history won five straight world titles.

PART II
PREPARING
TO RACE

CHAPTER 4

Train Harder to Improve Yourself

Toughness is building resistance to the stresses of running farther and faster.

—The Feeling of Effort—

Runners are, by nature, extremists. By carrying good ideas too far, we run them into the ground. We think if doing something is good, then doing more must be better, and doing twice as much must be best of all. When overdoing doesn't work as we had hoped, we fall prey to theorists who overstate the opposite case—and then over-react in that direction.

In recent years we've swung in training from all speed work to no speed, from no slow distance to all slow distance. We've been hurt at both extremes. We've reacted to overdoses of speed and distance by trying to eliminate all discomfort. We've swung from very hard to very easy running, from daring to cautious running. We've swung from tightly to loosely structured programs. Underlying them are the warnings: "Run as you feel, not by a schedule," and, "Listen to your body, not to your ego."

But your body often lies to you. If you waited until it was perfectly able and willing to run, you might not feel like training more than once or twice a week—and even then wouldn't take any chances.

The pendulum may now have swung as far as it will go in the direction of hang-loose ease. A natural move back toward the other extreme is due. Roger Robinson, a world-class masters athlete and a columnist for *New Zealand Runner* magazine, signals interest in movement toward harder work when he writes, "We runners are cautioned to cut back the workload, exercise without excess, slow down before [we] break down, run the short sweet way. I have one carefully considered and scientific comment on all this: It's garbage.

"Slow running trains you to run slowly. Low mileage produces low race quality. Easy running is fun, it's quite good for your health, and it's the right level of exercise for many people. But it won't narrow the gap between you and Said Aouita."

Robinson, who ran a sub-2:20 marathon after age 40 and a sub-2:30 after age 50, gives the run-as-you-feel theory equally blunt treatment. He says, "Deep inside, we're all work-shy. 'Listen to your body,' the experts keep telling us. Up to a point, they are right. But if I listened to my body, I'd never get through the first hard 400. If I listened to my body, I'd do repetition slow jogs past the bikinis [on the beach]. If I listened to my body, I'd live off toffee-pops and vintage port, and I'd look like Garfield." Robinson concludes that "inside this lean and hungry frame there lurks the soul of a plump idler on the fringes of life. Don't tell me to listen to my body. It's planning to turn me into a blob."

A main difference between true runners and dabblers at running is how often they obey the stop signs. You are a true runner because of the running you do on the days when you didn't feel like starting.

There also are days when feelings lie in reverse. You want to run when your body really needs to rest. But far more often you don't feel like taking the hardest step—the first one out the door—and look for reasons not to take it. These reasons usually have nothing to do with your ability to run. You just feel sleepy, hung over, harried, stuffy, or stiff—feelings that running is more likely to cure than to make worse.

Get past the lying feelings by making them wait to be heard. Plan only to start, reserve judgment for a mile or two, and only then decide where to go from there. The body tells the truth after it is warmed up. More often than not, the voices that conspired against running will have stilled by then.

—The Stress of Training—

Athletic training is a prescription item. It is essentially an exercise in balancing dosages of stress.

Stress isn't just an emotional condition of being wound too tightly or stretched too far, and it isn't all bad. In fact, the selective application of physical stress lies at the heart of all training techniques.

Stresses are a normal and natural part of living. They come from many directions—physical, emotional, social, and environmental—and in various combinations. We generally absorb these stresses into the pace of life. They become harmful only when they come in too heavy amounts for too long a time.

The human body is an amazingly pliable instrument. It adapts to almost any activity if you work into it gradually, and it balks only to protect itself from eventual destruction. Apply the proper stresses in the proper amounts, and you become a fitter athlete.

You're Tough Enough If. . .

▲ *You accept that racing long and fast requires training long and fast.*
▲ *You ignore the feelings that conspire to keep you from training.*
▲ *You know the difference between good stress and bad stress.*
▲ *You learn that stress is a prescription to take in proper doses.*
▲ *You calculate the effects of these doses by keeping a diary.*
▲ *You find your own best mixture of long, fast, and easy runs.*
▲ *You train up to longest-race distance but at a slower pace.*
▲ *You train up to fastest-race speed but at a shorter distance.*
▲ *You combine full speed with full distance only in the race.*
▲ *You treat the hardest training runs as race dress rehearsals.*

Understress, and you don't improve. Overstress, and your performances and perhaps even your health suffer.

Overstressing causes many illnesses and injuries. With runners, these often are self-inflicted—and therefore can be self-corrected. Dr. Hans Selye, a Canadian medical researcher, made the stress phenomenon his life's work. He observed that most diseases are symptoms of stress that a person can't handle, and that many of the physical break-downs of athletes come from this same source. "When we finished our laborious analysis of its nature," says Dr. Selye, "stress turned out to be something quite simple to understand. It is essentially the wear and tear in the body caused by life at any one time."

Selye notes that exposure to this wear and tear activates the body's defenses. The body has a reservoir of "adaptive energy" for handling everyday battering, plus a reserve supply for emergencies. But if the doses of stress are too heavy and prolonged, you no longer can adapt or even cope. The reserves are drained, and you go into what Selye calls the "exhaustion phase of the General Adaptation Syndrome." Symptoms then appear. The most common in runners are a sudden drop in performance, a quick change in weight, rapid pulse, disturbed sleep, anxiety and irritability, fatigue that lingers from one day to the next, colds and fever, and muscle and tendon pain. (Chapter 6 covers these warning signs in detail.)

According to Dr. Selye, "When superficial adaption energy is exhausted through exertion, it can slowly be restored from a deeper store during rest." But he warns that each time we ignore stress symptoms and the need to recover from them, we risk major damage.

So how does this theory translate into practical terms for a runner? Should you avoid stress? Not at all. If you're trying to improve, you must seek it out and push the thin line between enough and too much.

Think of yourself as a violin string. Like the string, you have a great capacity to perform. That potential is wasted when you lie limp and unused. Only when you're stretched properly can you fulfill your intended role. But that stretching can go too far. When pressures pull too hard in opposite directions, *snap*!

The trick is to find the ideal level of stress, the point of tautness that lets you perform while still holding some resiliency in reserve. Then when emergencies come up—either real ones in the form of unavoidable life crises, or artificial ones brought on by hard training and racing—you can meet them by stretching some more instead of snapping. Dr. Selye concludes, "The goal is certainly not to avoid stress. Stress is part of life. It is a natural by-product of all-out activity. There is no more justification for avoiding stress than for shunning food, exercise, or love. But in order to express yourself fully, you must find your optimum stress level."

—The Balancing of Work Loads—

Running for health is almost as simple as the sport's resident humorist Don Kardong once described it: "Just put one foot in front of the other. You can't get into too much trouble as long as you remember to alternate feet."

Running for sport isn't so simple. Like all sports, it requires learning a set of specialized skills by practicing them repeatedly. Training and racing require specific techniques if you are to maximize results and minimize risks.

The planning gets really tricky when you want the best of both worlds—to race well and to last a long time. You must run cautiously enough to stay healthy enough to keep going indefinitely. And you must train and race hard enough to stay happy with your performances. Therein lies a basic conflict. The running that keeps you healthy may not make you happy, and the running that makes you happy may not keep you healthy.

The healthiest runners obey Dr. Kenneth Cooper's formula: two to three miles a day, three to five days a week, all at a comfortable pace. Beyond these limits of distance, frequency, and intensity, the risk of injury escalates. However, the happiest runners seem to be the racers. Their fun *starts* at the point where Dr. Cooper would advise them to stop. To find the fun, they take the risks.

If you only want to run for health, don't race. If you aren't looking beyond this season's racing, train and race as if there's no next year. But if you want to race *and* survive, then steer a middle course. Do some health running and some thrill-seeking running, but all of neither.

Thriving as a racer requires going harder on the hard days—longer, faster, or both together—than a pure exerciser would ever go. Surviving as a runner requires taking easier easy days—and more of them—than a pure racer would dare take. This compromise course may leave you less healthy than a pure exerciser and less athletic than a pure athlete. But you also may stay happier than the fittest exercisers and healthier than the fastest racers.

The training formula outlined in this chapter balances the conflicting goals of short-term performance and long-term health. This formula gives running a split personality: half sport, half exercise. The two sides are unequal in size but equally important. They add up to one complete and lasting running experience.

For Tatyana Kazankina (number 10, from the Soviet Union), toughness meant being a woman far ahead of her time. Her final world records for 1500 and 3000 meters have stood since the early 1980s, and she's the only female to win the Olympic 1500 twice.

—The Mixture of Ingredients—

Never mind what the entry blank says about date, time, and place of your next race. It doesn't start at the starting line. It begins the day you make the decision to enter and the commitment to train. How well you do on race day is the product of what you start doing now.

Start by finding a race that challenges you. Racing is meant to take you beyond the familiar surroundings and comforts of everyday running. Look for a new way to explore the sport's vast opportunities, and to extend your own frontiers of distance and speed.

Fill out an entry blank and pay your fee. Most major events require you to sign up early. But even if they don't, this act of putting your name on the line and a check in the mail seals your commitment to train.

Now think about that training. You know the general rules of running, so I will talk here only about race preparation. It demands specific techniques to maximize results and minimize risks. Millions of words have been written and spoken on this subject. These can be reduced to three essentials in any racer's training program:

1. *Long:* Train long enough to prepare you for the distance of your longest race, which probably is much farther than you run day by day.
2. *Fast:* Train fast enough to prepare you for the pace of your fastest (and shortest) race, which probably is much faster than your everyday runs.
3. *Easy:* Train easy enough to let you recover fully between the long and the fast training sessions and races, which probably takes much more time than you think.

A set of "ones" deals with each of these three essential pieces in the running puzzle.

- *One long run, maximum, a week*...one hour or more, up to the length of the longest upcoming race...at least one minute per mile slower than race pace for this distance...optional one-minute-per-mile walking breaks on extralong runs.
- *One fast run, maximum, a week*...one mile or more, taken straight or interval-style ...at least one minute per mile faster than easy training pace, up to the speed of the shortest upcoming race.
- *One easy day, minimum, after each long or fast run*...one hour maximum (including time spent dressing, stretching, and showering)...at least one minute per mile slower than race pace for this distance.

"Long" and "fast" combine as races some weeks. In that case, take either one easy week or one day per mile raced—whichever period is longer—before going long or fast again.

The "week" doesn't need to contain a standard seven days. Each cycle can expand or contract as needed to fill with one long and one fast day (or both together as a race), and one or more easy or rest days between the hard ones.

These "ones" form the generic training plan that follows.

—The Easy Day's Run—

Easy, that last word in the training recipe, may be the most important and least appreciated. More races are lost by training too long and fast, too often, than by running too little or too easily.

The hardest training for most runners to schedule is the easiest kind. In few other sports is effort so directly linked with accomplishment, so running naturally attracts workaholics. They then are force-fed the most damaging myth in athletics and fitness: "Pain equals gain."

Racing can be—maybe even *should be*—uncomfortable, and some training must be directed at immunizing yourself against discomfort. You can't improve without it. But no one can stand to train painfully all the time. In that case, all pain equals is ever-increasing pain—until finally it breaks the runner down physically or psychologically.

Exciting and challenging as it might be, racing (as well as training that mimics the race in distance or speed) is an unnatural act. It tears you down, and you must build back up after hard efforts by taking easier ones.

Alternately tearing and repairing will eventually make you a better racer, but only if the recovery time between hard efforts is adequate. In other words, the easy running makes the hard work *work*.

Elite athletes have the capacity to alternate hard and easy days. However, most of us are slower to rebound. One or two hard sessions each week, in the form of an actual race or racelike speed or distance work, are about all we can tolerate.

Recovery doesn't demand complete rest, though taking at least one day off does have merit. You can recover while still satisfying the urge to keep running regularly.

Just remember to stay well within the comfort zone on these days. This may mean running a half-hour to an hour at one to two minutes per mile slower than current shortest-distance (that is to say, fastest) race pace. Older and less experienced runners who recover slower shouldn't feel guilty about staying on the low/slow end of that scale or doing even less.

Everyday running isn't the place to increase the length or intensity of training. Save that for the big days.

The easy runs are the meat and potatoes of the running diet. The dessert comes as small, infrequent portions of racing and training at abnormal speeds and distances.

—The Long Day's Run—

Distance is in the eye of the beholder. One runner's long race may be another's speed test. Elite athletes who average 15 to 20 miles a day aren't bothered much even by the marathon distance. Running that far *fast* is their main concern and the major focus of their training.

Experienced racers with less ambition and mileage feel the same way about events lasting less than an hour. They regularly go this far on everyday runs, so their aim in racing is to run these distances faster than usual.

Only when the race distance far exceeds your everyday limits do longer-than-normal training runs become critical. How long? It depends entirely on your goal.

Let's say you're aiming to run a first marathon (the tips that follow can be scaled down to whatever your longest racing distance might be). Estimate what your race time might be, then work up to that level on your long training runs.

You project a 3:30 marathon, for example. That 3½ hours becomes your training target. Work up to it by no more than half-hour steps, starting one above your current longest run. If that is 1½ hours, go up to two hours the next time.

If the amounts and the progress rates sound imposing, consider a technique that strikes many runners as heresy but that actually works. Take walking breaks of perhaps one minute per mile during the longest runs. You can instantly double your longest nonstop distance this way. If you don't like the word "walk," think of it as another application of interval training—which breaks a large chunk of work into smaller pieces to make them more manageable.

Aim to eliminate all walking on race day. But if you still need the breaks, take them. The time they cost you doesn't matter. Only getting to the finish line does.

Go long before you think of going fast. Only if the racing distance seems short do you need to concern yourself with training for speed.

—The Fast Day's Run—

Adding distance is a matter of persistence, of doing more running at the same old pace. Increasing speed is a technical problem, requiring a change of style.

We illustrated distance training with the marathon, the top of most runners' racing range. Our speed example is the 5-K, the shortest and fastest road event for most of us.

Five kilometers is a speed test many runners fail because they suffer from what might be called "one-pace syndrome." They simply never have learned to run fast. Runners with little background in short-distance racing may never have picked up the techniques (more spring from the ankles, more lift with the knees, longer stride, greater arm action, etc.). So they can't go much faster in races than in training, or in 5-Ks than in marathons.

Fortunately, runners who have done the least speed work can improve the most by doing a small amount of it. As little as one fast mile a week for several weeks can lead to an improvement of a half-minute or more in a 5-K race.

If you're looking for a speed breakthrough, go to a track or an accurately measured stretch of flat road once a week for two or more weeks in a row. Warm up well, then time yourself for a mile. Try to run at least one minute, but not more than two minutes, faster than your everyday pace.

Say your daily running averages 8:00 miles. Do this mile in 6:00 to 7:00. Go fast, but don't try to simulate a race. Finish the mile thinking you might be able to go several more miles at this rate when the time is right.

You don't need to limit your speed work to a single, nonstop mile. Vary the routine by running longer at race pace, or by splitting up the fast run interval-style (with recovery breaks inserted).

But still keep the total modest. Limit the fast training to one-half your race distance.

The purpose of speed training is to rehearse full racing pace at a partial distance. Long training simulates the full distance at a slower pace. Combine full distance at full pace only when it counts: in the race itself.

—The Dress-Rehearsal Day—

May all your race day surprises be pleasant ones. The best surprise you can give yourself is to run farther or faster than you ever have before. Yet even that type of result shouldn't surprise you too much. After all, hadn't you trained with that improvement in mind?

During the longest and fastest training runs, you rehearse the experiences and stresses of the race so they won't come as unpleasant shocks on race day. You test yourself separately for distance and speed.

Long tests, run at race length but at a slower pace, acquaint you with the feeling of covering the full distance. Fast tests, run at race pace but at partial distance, introduce you to the mechanics of moving at full speed. You blend the two factors in the race.

Testing doesn't end with distance and pace. These dress rehearsals serve many other purposes, all designed to immunize you against rude surprises. Very little that happens to you on race day should be happening for the first time then. So don't just simulate the race in training. Mimic the whole race day, paying special attention to the following four concerns:

1. *What you consume.* Experiment with adjustments to prerace diet before race day. Test the timing, makeup, and amount of your eating and drinking.

    If a food seems to help you on test days, keep it in the race routine. If it bothers you now, avoid it later. If you do better by skipping a meal before running hard, don't eat.

    What you eat in the last meal tends to have mostly negative effects. What you drink before and during a long run can positively affect performance and protect health. Practice taking the same liquids at the same intervals in long tests as you'll be served on race day.

2. *What you wear.* The cardinal rule is "nothing new on race day." This applies most specifically to the shoes.

    You're tempted to run in the lightest possible footwear, thinking that every ounce of weight shed converts into seconds saved. This may be true—in theory.

    In fact, you give up protection at a time when impact stress increases. The cost may be discomfort at best, an injury at worst.

    When adding distance, speed, or both, stick with the shoes you know you can trust. Only use shoes in long and fast training that worked in easy runs, and only use those in races that have passed the harder tests.

For Ingrid Kristiansen (Norway), toughness has meant doing her best racing since becoming a mother. While raising a son, she has collected an unprecedented triple: world records for 5000 meters, 10,000 meters, and marathon.

The "nothing new" rule extends to clothing. Dress for tests as you would for a race. Do your experimenting on test days, not race days.

3. *When you race.* Most road races, for practical reasons of traffic and temperature, start in the early to mid-morning. This time causes problems if you normally aren't fully awake until noon or if you don't generally run until sundown.

You can't change the starting time, so rearrange your schedule on test days. If the race starts at eight A.M., test at eight o'clock. Unpleasant as this sounds, get out of bed two hours earlier and perhaps take a shower *before* running to speed the wake-up process.

Morning runners face a different set of problems on those rare occasions of afternoon or evening races. You aren't used to waiting all day to run or to planning your afternoon activities around a run, and most of all you aren't adapted to the warmer temperatures of afternoon.

Delay your tests until the hour of the race. Experience all of the unusual conditions and find ways to cope with them.

4. *Where you race.* Familiarity breeds confidence. If you know what to expect from a racecourse, you're more confident that you can run it well.

Test yourself on the actual course or on a close facsimile. Match the surface, terrain, and surroundings of race day as closely as possible.

Test for road racing on the roads, for cross-country over the country, for track on the track. If the race has hills, practice running up and down hills of the same steepness and number. Familiarity also breeds competence.

—The Specifics of Training—

"Getting More from Less Training" read the title of this seminar. While a panel of supposed experts expounded on the subject, a true expert sat quietly in the audience. Norm Green from Pennsylvania would run a 2:27:42 marathon the next day, at age 55. No one gets more from his training miles than Green does. He averages less than 60 miles a week, and he rarely trains more than 10 miles at a time. But he does all his training at or near marathon race pace (sub-6:00 miles) and takes his longest runs in races.

More-from-less does not mean something-for-nothing. Green clearly is a hard worker, as well as an efficient one who makes every mile serve a specific purpose. Few runners train as specifically for racing as Green does. And few of us could tolerate miniraces as often as he runs them. But in Green's success lies a lesson in a tongue-twisting physiological concept: specificity of effort. In running terms, the rule states that as you train, so shall you race.

Green can handle exceptionally specific training. But most runners can't race as often as he does without getting hurt. For them, slow daily runs serve a purpose: not as training for speed but recovery from it.

The easiness also has penalties, as Hal Higdon once noted in a *Runner's World* article. A successful competitor for more than 30 years, he writes, "I'm inclined to believe that runners are more susceptible to injuries when we train less, simply because cutting back leaves us unprepared for our inevitable excesses: those long runs and races that I, for one, have no intention of abandoning."

The most specific training for racing *is* racing. Next-best is training at race pace for a portion of the distance, as Green does. If you want to race well, you must race often—but not too often.

Racing, like hard training, is a prescription item. The trick is finding the proper dosage between too much and too little. Overracing is exhausting and often injurious. Underracing hurts in more subtle ways, as sluggishness in the race and soreness afterward from being ill prepared.

Two prescriptions are generally recommended and widely followed. One uses a percentage of total mileage, the other a number of recovery days. The first prescription suggests limiting racing and racelike training to 10 percent of total mileage. The second advises taking one easy day for each mile of latest race. (Neither gives a minumum figure, though there surely is one below which racing suffers.)

However, these are only the broadest of guidelines. Find the dosage that fits you best.

—The Records You Keep—

Someone else's writing can only put you on the starting line. From there, you must go your own way—then tell what you did there. A diary helps give your life stories happier endings.

You don't even have to write many, if any, words in the diary. Its numbers alone tell stories as they recall old training sessions and suggest new possibilities.

Follow three guidelines for record keeping: keep it simple, keep it up, and keep it.

Keep It Simple

Limit the amount of information to a few essentials that can be listed briefly, quickly, and in accessible form for review. The harder it is to maintain a diary, the less likely you are to use it.

Where you put the records isn't as important as which ones you keep. Preprinted running diaries, those with blanks to fill in, appeal to some runners. But these books aren't necessary, or necessarily practical. They may ask you for too much information, too little, or the wrong type.

A calendar with large blocks of white space will work nicely as long as it is tacked on your bedroom or office wall. But the calendar doesn't travel or store well.

A notebook works best as a portable, permanent record. Fill it at the rate of one, two, or a few lines a day.

List the month across the top of the page, the date down the left side. Record the run's length (in distance, time, or both), and then note any extraordinary events (such as races and race-effort training results, or episodes of injury and illness).

If you can't control your urge to write more, keep a journal on separate daily pages. But still put only the runs on your monthly summary page. This is the heart of your record keeping.

Keep It Up

Days of training leave behind what appear to be random footprints in the diary. You can't take much direction from them at first. But the weeks, months, and years form a trail that points two ways. It shows where you have been and where you might go next.

The longer you maintain the diary, the clearer become your patterns of response to the exercise. And the clearer will be your thinking about it.

Analyze the acccumulating data over extended periods of time to judge your results. Make the accounting by the month, not the week. Weeks are too short. One unusual day can make a week look far better or worse than it really was, yet have little training effect one way or the other. A month's time flattens out these pseudohighs and lows. The longer period shows more realistically what you've accomplished and how you've failed.

Months come in different sizes, all of them large. Instead of quoting confusing mileage or time totals, think in terms of daily averages and count only the actual running days in that figure so as not to penalize yourself for taking necessary days off.

Weekly mileage is the most overrated figure in running. The percentage of racing is the most underrated.

Racelike efforts (and these include extrafast and extralong training) are as risky as they are exciting. They must be taken in small doses.

Your prescription depends on your ability to bounce back from hard efforts. Start finding your ideal dosage by comparing the monthly total of racelike work with the quality of races and the incidence of problems. You'll see a pattern as the months add up.

Calculate the daily average and racing percentage at the bottom of each month's page. Note, too, the longest and fastest runs of the month (an indication of your current distance and speed limits).

Review the highest and lowest points of your month, and ask yourself why you hit each. Use the answers to promote the ups and eliminate the downs in months to come.

Keep It

Store your records in a safe place, treating them as the precious volumes they will become in time. Their value grows along with their age and bulk.

──CHAPTER 5──

Train Smarter to Protect Yourself

Toughness is knowing when to progress by pushing on and by backing off.

─The Hard/Easy System─

The least you can say about Bill Bowerman is that he's one of America's all-time great track coaches, if not the greatest. He coached four national championship teams and flocks of sub-four-minute-milers at the University of Oregon, and once served as U.S. Olympic coach. However, Bowerman's influence reaches far beyond coaching elite athletes to touch runners on every level. He laid early groundwork for America's running boom by importing the run-for-fitness message of New Zealander Arthur Lydiard in the 1960s and coauthoring the first best-selling book on this subject, *Jogging*. Bowerman then designed shoes that would keep the masses of new runners safe and comfortable.

His most lasting gift to health, fitness, and performance is the hard/easy system of training. You can't improve without hard work, Bowerman says. But working hard every day will destroy you. Every training program that works now mixes hard and easy days. Bowerman gets due credit from others for this concept, but he asks little for himself. He has talked and written sparingly about the roots of his system.

He made an exception when telling of a former pupil who was to become as widely known as his coach. This story deals with Olympic marathoner and prominent writer Kenny Moore. Bowerman says that as a sophomore at Oregon, "Moore was a problem. He'd hooked up with the seductive idea that the more he ran, the better he'd be. On Sundays, when I asked him to cover 20 miles, he'd do 30. And on easy days, when I thought three miles and a swim was enough, he'd sneak in 12. The

---

You're Tough Enough If. . .

▲ *You balance the conflicting goals of good racing and good health.*
▲ *You improve not just by training harder, but also by training smarter.*
▲ *You realize that easy running and rest make the hard work* work.
▲ *You limit yourself to a day or two of hard work each week.*
▲ *You take at least one easy day after each hard day of training.*
▲ *You take at least one easy day after each* mile *that you race.*
▲ *You tiptoe along the comfort/discomfort border in everyday running.*
▲ *You toe the line between discomfort and destruction in races.*
▲ *You ease the pressures of time by making friends with the clock.*
▲ *You build seasonal hard/easy cycles into your running year.*

---

result was perfectly plain to me: he was sick and hurt all the time, and of no use to the team."

Moore's two-mile time had slowed from a best of 9:12 to 9:48 when Bowerman told him this overstressing had to stop. "From then on, I would watch him perform his easy-day run. It was to be three miles on the grass, seven minutes a mile. I told him I had spies who would report any midnight runs, and such reports were cause for suspension from the team. He told me I was a tyrant. He remembers, at this hazy distance, that we had this talk while he was hanging from his neck by my affectionate grip. But remember, this was a man who went on to earn his living by his imagination."

After three weeks of getting the rest he needed, Moore ran the two-mile a full minute faster than he'd done while overworking. He dropped his personal best by 24 seconds. Moore told his coach, "I still think you're a tyrant. And thank God for that!"

Moore became a believer in the hard/easy system that day but still had occasional lapses of faith. One came a year later. "In 1965, he won both the steeplechase and the three-mile in our conference meet," says the coach. "That was a lot of stress. The next day, I told him to cut his long run to 10 miles. Naturally, he set out to do 20. At 10¼ miles, he suffered a stress fracture in his foot. I hated to lose him for the NCAA meet. But I have to admit that I was proud of myself for setting his limit so accurately."

Bowerman knows runners. He knows that our greatest strength—our will to endure—can also be our biggest weakness. He knows that we run into more trouble from going too far, too often, than from not doing enough. He knows, too, that "the most progress is made not by the man or woman who trains the most, but the one who trains *most intelligently*. This means you need a careful sense of your responses to individual stress levels."

You need to know the difference between enough and too much. You sometimes need to become the type of "tyrant" Bill Bowerman was with Kenny Moore, to protect yourself from yourself.

For Billy Mills (left, from the United States), toughness meant overcoming impoverished beginnings on an Indian reservation, a lackluster college career, and finally the overwhelming odds against him to win the 1964 Olympic 10,000.

— The Science of Recovery —

Dr. David Costill was delivering his fourth talk in 24 hours. He'd given the first three to employees of a major insurance company and now he was speaking to runners at a 10-K race.

This work load hadn't tired Dr. Costill. He was still doing what he was first to do in this sport. With a pleasing blend of scientific calm and missionary zeal, he translated findings from his Human Performance Laboratory at Ball State University into road-worthy lessons for runners.

Costill's white hair befit his position as running's senior physiologist but belied the fact that he was reliving his athletic youth, only better. When running hurt his knees a few years earlier, he returned to his original sport of swimming. He would swim faster times 30 years later than he did at Ohio University in the 1950s.

In his early 50s, he was easing back into running. He pointed a finger at himself while saying, "One major fault of runners is our strong work ethic. We suffer from too much motivation." He described a "vicious cycle that traps runners. First, we train too much. Then we start performing poorly. When this happens, we think the only answer is to train even harder. And we perform even worse."

Dr. Costill told of a longtime colleague from his lab. "He gradually builds up his mileage until he gets hurt, which usually happens at about 80 miles a week. Then he starts the cycle all over again. He's been training that way for 20 years."

His topic this night: "How Much Is Enough?" He said that most serious runners probably would stay healthier and compete better by training less. "I often hear these days about runners who take up the triathlon, and suddenly their running improves," said Costill. "They say it's because of the cross-training effect. I say it's simply because they've cut back on their running to make room for the other two sports."

He noted the big difference between running and most other aerobic sports: "the pounding." It shortens the safe mileage and lengthens the recovery time between hard runs.

Dr. Costill identified the two keys to success in running as "developing a big aerobic capacity and having plenty of fuel on board." Running lots of miles boosts aerobic potential, and glycogen acts as the main fuel of working muscles.

He flashed slides of his lab tests that show how runners' aerobic capacities increase dramatically up to weekly mileages of 50 to 60. "Physiologically," said Costill, "you're probably not going to gain much beyond that point. You may continue to gain psychologically from the extra miles, but at the risk of beating yourself up." The higher the mileage, the more exhausted the legs feel. Injuries rates to dead legs may climb, but even if they don't the extra training is often unproductive. Costill explained why: "When runners train more than about 50 or 60 miles a week, they can't store enough fuel. When they train too hard, too often, they're chronically depleted of glycogen."

He recommended holding total weekly mileage below 60, training down for longer periods before and after races, and fueling up the muscles through adjustments in both training and diet.

Dr. Costill's research indicates that runners may need to taper up to three weeks before a major race in order to restore full bounciness to the legs. A marathoner, for instance, might schedule the last long run that far in advance.

He doesn't expect us to train down that long before every race, of course, because that would leave a regular racer no time for anything but tapering. Costill does advise "reducing training and eating foods high in carbohydrates the last 72 hours" before most events.

Based on studies in his lab, he has simplified the carbohydrate-loading that fills muscles with glycogen. His routine does away with the traditional depletion run and low-carbo phase, and goes directly to the fun part.

Dr. Costill said that recovery after a race is "tapering in reverse." Repay the fatigue debt with three days to three weeks of light training, and refuel glycogen-starved legs with more carbos.

—The Edge of Discomfort—

You possess a low-tech but highly sophisticated system for balancing stress loads. It doesn't rely on any scientific devices or formulas. It's the free and priceless tool called body wisdom. The body will tell you all you need to know about how much is enough or too much, if you only pay attention. That's the view or Dr. George Sheehan, one of running's most trusted advisors, whose pet phrase is "listen to your body."

"The body knows better than any single test what you should do," says Dr. Sheehan. "You don't need to put technology between yourself and your body. You simply set your inner dial just below the discomfort zone, then stay there—easing off the pace whenever it starts to hurt and increasing it when it feels too easy. What feels right *is* right."

Pain is the body's first line of defense—its natural warning system—and you ignore it at your peril. Dr. Sheehan talks of pushing the comfort/discomfort borderline.

Ian Jackson calls it "playing the edge." Jackson is the George Sheehan or Kenneth Cooper of stretching. Jackson's *Yoga and the Athlete* was every bit as revolutionary a book, despite much smaller sales, as Dr. Cooper's first *Aerobics* or Dr. Sheehan's *On Running*. Cooper and Sheehan wrote that the way to train most effectively is steadily and gently, not briefly and violently. Jackson gives similar advice about stretching exercises, and he helped wean runners from herky-jerky calisthenics.

On one level, the yoga book offers specific how-to advice. But on a higher level, it describes one man's journey away from the pain-equals-gain school of training to a more humane—and ultimately more productive—approach.

Jackson repeatedly urges exercisers to "play the edge." This principle makes yoga as different from traditional calisthenics as easy distance running is from intensive interval training.

Old-style calisthenics rely on quick, repeated movements. They attack pain barriers in a self-defeating way. A muscle jerked into extension, beyond the point of pain, responds by jerking back. This reflex action tightens and perhaps even injures the muscle that the exercise was supposed to stretch and protect.

In the yoga approach, you gently nudge the barrier of pain instead of attacking it. You stretch slowly, find the "edge" of discomfort, back off slightly, then hold at that point for several seconds. The first thing you notice during the "hold" is that, by letting yourself relax, you ease into a longer stretch than was possible under tension. You notice after a few weeks of stretching this way that the edge has moved to a point you couldn't have reached earlier without great pain. You now stretch to it comfortably.

Whatever your exercise is, this rule applies. It works as well for running training as it does for stretching.

Playing the edge with running pace means finding that invisible, ever-shifting line between comfort and discomfort, backing off a bit, and then holding the effort steady at just below that borderline. The pace may vary widely from day to day, or even within a single run, but the effort remains constant.

As you play the edge repeatedly, it moves. When it does, you're able to run comfortably at a pace that earlier had been a pain.

If you'd never nudged the pain barrier, you wouldn't have moved it farther out. If you'd tried to crash it with brute force, it would have broken you.

In the long run, you gain more from listening carefully to the body's signals of discomfort than from trying to muffle its screams of pain.

The advice in this chapter applies to everyday running. Races and the specific long and fast training that mimics racing are, of course, somewhat painful.

However, an "edge" still applies to race efforts. Only now, instead of nudging the border between comfortable and uncomfortable, you tiptoe along a higher line between discomfort and destruction.

— The Part-Time Athlete —

"To be a good runner," remarked one who was racing his best ever at age 40, "you must be single, unemployed, or both." He was newly divorced and worked less than two weeks each month as an international airline pilot.

Bill Rodgers would agree with the employment part of that statement. This professional runner has expressed doubts that anyone his age who worked a 40-hour week could ever beat him.

Good running takes time. Those of us who never seem to have enough of it envy people like Rodgers and the pilot. They enjoy the luxury of scheduling their days around their runs instead of squeezing their running into a crowded schedule.

Anyone with world-class ambitions must treat running as a job, giving it full time and attention. Professionals and would-be pros can and must take the time to do everything right in running.

One such pro makes sure she gets enough sleep, waking at a civilized hour each morning. She lives on a hillside but worries about hills causing injuries, so she drives down to the flatlands to train. She stretches carefully before and after running. This full-time runner supplements her twice-daily runs with Nautilus work. Between training sessions, she may visit her physician, chiropractor, physiologist, or masseur. These activities occupy her whole day.

Such commitment to physical perfection is to be admired—but not imitated by people with more pressing commitments than running. The athletes you read about most are those least like yourself.

You don't need to be told to spend more time on your sport. You need to be shown how to use your limited time better.

Reg Harris wrote and self-published a book with that purpose in mind. He now lives in California but in the early 1970s coached in Tunisia. He helped prepare three-time Olympic medalist Mohamed Gammoudi for the Munich Games. Harris says the Tunisians taught him one major lesson: "Train *smarter*, not harder. I became convinced that too many Americans have gone mileage-crazy. They have forgotten—or never learned—that excellent results can be achieved with relatively low mileage."

When Harris came home from his tour of duty as Tunisia's national coach, he began working with runners from the opposite end of the spectrum. He taught jogging and road running classes at a college, and coached high school and junior high teams.

Before starting to write his book, Harris asked potential readers what they wanted to know that they hadn't already learned from dozens of running books and hundreds of magazine articles. The main thrust of their replies: tell us how to run *better*, not more. A man who averaged sub-six-minute miles in his 10-K races wrote, "I'd like to see more information on how to make the most of a 20- to 40-mile training week for those of us who can't spare the time for more running." A woman marathoner who was fast enough to qualify for Boston said, "There's too much stuff [written] for the serious marathoner. I wish writers would deal with the real world, the runner who juggles job and running and still has time for a family."

These responses prompted Reg Harris to coin the phrase "part-time runner" and to use it as his book title. He writes, "Perhaps the best definition of a part-time runner is that he or she enjoys running and racing, but only as part of a busy life. While running does have a high priority, it is seldom the most important thing in his or her life. Most part-time runners must accomplish their goals in a limited amount of time and with a limited amount of energy."

—The Hour Each Day—

My subject here is time management. Making time to run and using that time well.

Runners who are only looking for exercise aren't troubled much by time constraints. They train two or three miles every other day, totaling only a couple of hours a week running. Almost anyone can spare that little time. The problem develops when this quota no longer satisfies you. When you run twice as far and twice as often, the total mileage is still quite modest by the standards of serious part-time runners. But you already have *quadrupled* the time requirement.

If you train for marathons and add total-fitness activities to your routine, the sport can take up almost as much time as a second job. Even if that investment doesn't bother you, consider your family and boss. They probably aren't as tolerant of the time drain.

Running too much at the expense of higher priorities is one common pitfall facing the busy runner. The other comes from the opposite direction: running too little, too fast in order to substitute quality for quantity. Even if you're lucky enough to escape injury in the second case, the run becomes just another extension of the day's rat race instead of a break from it.

A solution to the time problem is the one that applies to many other training and racing puzzles: strike the proper balance between enough and too much. That's so easy to say, but so hard to do!

Anyone can fall back on the excuse, "I'm too busy to run. I don't have the time."

No one is given the time. You can only give it to yourself. If you really want to run, you find the time for it.

Give yourself a full hour a day. Schedule one hour in 24 that is yours alone, to do with what you wish. Why an hour? Because that's long enough to hold your standard weekday/workday running and long enough so you won't be tempted to run too fast. Yet an hour is still short enough to fit into most daily schedules without straining them.

Fit your day's run into that hour, but seldom take longer than that. Treat the hour as your island of calm and stability in a turbulent day.

Taking time for yourself has great value even if you don't fill it with running. The busier you are, the more you need to take this break from the other obligations of the day.

You're still left with 15 or so waking hours for taking care of those duties. You'll take care of them better if you give yourself this break.

—The Time-Saving Plan—

My time-saving plan has three simple components: make time to run, make friends with time, and make best use of time.

Make Time to Run

When you run depends on the time of day when you operate best and when it's easiest for you to make time available for running. You might make it by waking up earlier in the morning, watching one less TV show at night, or skipping lunch at noon.

Runners who favor the first-thing-each-morning routine point to these advantages: seldom do other people or activities interfere at that time of day, you wake up more quickly by getting your day off to a running start, and the traffic is lightest and air is coolest and cleanest then.

Runners who prefer the evening say they feel loosest and most awake then. Training at that hour relieves the day's tensions and frustrations.

Runners with an hour off from work at lunchtime may find the time is better spent running than eating. The run temporarily blunts your appetite, provides a physical break from mental fatigue, and helps keep you alert all afternoon.

Schedule your hour at the most convenient, or least inconvenient, time.

For Rosa Mota (left, from Portugal), toughness has meant becoming the most consistent winner in women's marathon history. Between 1982 and 1990, she collected three European titles, a world championship, and an Olympic gold medal.

Make Friends with Time

Run with the clock, not against it. Apart from special time trials and races, forget about how far you run and think only about how much time you spend running. Count minutes, not miles.

Why run by time? The practical advantage is freedom from the time-consuming job of designing and measuring courses. You're no longer obliged to follow those routes step by step.

You're free to alter old paths and explore new ones while filling the allotted time. Minutes pass at the same rate wherever you run them, and an accurate measurement is right there on your wrist.

The bigger reward from time-running is more subtle. Switching to the time standard relieves the pressure of trying to fight time. The natural tendency when running a set distance is to finish it as quickly as possible, which often means pushing yourself too hard.

However, you can't make a period of time pass any faster. In fact, it seems to take longer when you try to rush it. So the natural tendency here is to run the time at a comfortable pace.

Make Best Use of Time

Richard Watson, author of The Philosopher's Diet (which is more of a running book than a nutrition text), recommends splitting the hour this way: "Ten minutes to get ready, 30 on the road, 20 to shower and dress."

If you're a fast dresser, you can run more, but the advice remains the same: fit the run loosely into the daily hour. Run at least half an hour of it, but stop short of an hour most days.

Run from your front door instead of driving someplace else to start and spending the transit time unproductively. Warm up for running by running slowly, not with supplemental exercises of dubious merit.

Keep the time of day and the time spent running fairly constant. But vary what you do within that time.

When you run by time, your pace self-adjusts to your feelings that day. Yet you still finish on schedule, no matter whether you went nearly all-out or at a near-walk.

This time period also allows informal speed training. Add small amounts of faster running while still observing the earlier warning against trying to crowd the limited time of weekday/workday runs with too much fast work.

Fred Wilt, one of America's first writers on training topics, once suggested a quick session for busy runners: a warm-up mile or two plus another mile of alternate fast and slow 100-meter intervals. A slight variation on Wilt's workout, to fit our time theme, would be to run one minute fast and one slow for the final 10 minutes.

Save the formal speedwork, longer runs, and races for weekends and vacations. Limit these time-gobbling sessions to days when you have extra hours to spend driving to a special site, socializing with other runners, and recovering from the unusual effort. A busy runner doesn't have many days like this. When they come, treat them as luxury items. The modest runs in between are the necessities.

—The Breaks that Heal—

Getting hurt or getting sick can be a lucky break. It can ruin a runner's season but make the next one even better. Consider the examples of Mary Decker Slaney, America's all-time best track woman, and Dick Beardsley, the country's second-fastest marathoner.

Decker hadn't yet added her new last name in 1981. But she had just added a new scar, this one on an Achilles tendon that had been damaged in a European race the previous summer. The tendon was healing on schedule, but an old shin problem had returned. Mary wasn't running. She had an appointment that afternoon with her orthopedic surgeon. When she came back from that visit, she was in tears. Her face gave the news before her voice did: another operation due, then another three to six months of recovery before she could race seriously again. There went her track racing for the year.

Dick Beardsley wasn't running in late 1981. He explained that a pack of dogs had ganged up on him while he was on a long run. No bites had landed, but the dogs had knocked Beardsley off his feet. At nearly six feet tall and less than 130 pounds of weight, he has few fat pads. Dick fell hard on a bony hip and later developed a case of sciatica that lasted for months. There went his road racing for the year.

The next year, 1982, Beardsley managed a couple of good training months before the Boston Marathon. Decker had about the same amount of time to prepare for the indoor season. That was long enough for both of them.

Mary set indoor world records in almost every race she ran that winter. Never had a runner, male or female, so thoroughly dominated a season.

Dick ran a 2:08:54 marathon at Boston. Among Americans, only Alberto Salazar (who beat him by only two seconds that day) had ever done better.

It might be argued that Decker and Beardsley did so well *despite* their physical problems of a few months before. I say they may have done so well *because* they had been hurt. Forced layoffs often carry such disguised blessings.

Voluntary breaks carry the same benefits. All runners need holidays from hard training and racing, and we're wise not to wait for nature to demand them with injuries and illnesses.

Jeff Galloway, a former Olympic runner and now a popular running writer and speaker, suggests a plan of this type. He recommends not only mixing harder and easier days (as coach Bill Bowerman advises in this chapter), but also applying that principle to longer periods of time. Galloway recommends slacking off once in a while to pull yourself out of a "fatigue debt." The formula he uses himself is one easy week in every four.

Jeff doesn't take that week completely off. He likes to run too much to do that. But he does cut out all racing, and all long and fast running in that week. He says he comes back from this minivacation stronger than if he'd pushed through that week at normal mileage and pace.

The hard/easy mixture can also extend to months. Emiel Puttemans, a Belgian who once held world records at several distances, spent a month each year doing what he wouldn't let himself do the rest of the year. He ran once a day, if that. He stayed out late at night and slept in the next morning. He ate heavily and let himself gain weight without feeling guilt. Then when the month was up, he was eager to return to his normal training habits.

Author Tom Osler stretches hard/easy even more. He alternates high and low seasons of the year. Some top athletes alternate whole years of high and low intensity.

No one has carried hard/easy further than Lasse Viren. He ran easily for three years, then hammered the Olympic year. Viren's peaks were quite short. The valleys in between were long and deep. He once said, "It's not possible to conserve good form for a long time in distance running. But top shape can be planned and timed fairly accurately."

Viren sometimes couldn't even win local races in off-years. Yet he collected two gold medals in two straight Olympics.

—The High-Low Cycles—

Tom Osler is one of the brightest thinkers in running. His *Conditioning of Distance Runners*, published in 1966, was one of the first great advice booklets and he expanded on its themes in the full-length *Serious Runner's Handbook* (1978).

Osler was so slow and thick-legged in his early running days that friends called him "Turtle." Yet he stretched his limited genetic gifts into national championships at distances from 25 kilometers to 50 miles. He broke 2½ hours for the marathon when that time was still national-class. More importantly, Osler—a mathematician by profession—took an analytical approach to running and wrote out his analyses. One of his hidden gems deals with the seasonal ups and downs of long-distance racers.

These are as normal and natural, he says, as the shifts from summer to fall and winter to spring. "One can rarely maintain a high performance level for more than three months. Heavy racing must therefore be terminated after about three months or when symptoms of energy depletion are first observed." (See those symptoms in chapter 6.)

Osler thinks that if you hit a peak in the first month, you'll probably bottom out in the fourth, then climb all the way out of that valley and back to the top by the sixth month. He says that you can reach higher peaks and weather the valleys better by cooperating with these cycles than by fighting them.

Osler found during his own best years of racing that each year fell neatly into two cycles lasting about six months apiece. Each cycle held a "high" period of about three months and a "low" of the same length. He raced best and stayed healthiest if he emphasized his racing and harder training at the high times and avoided these stresses during the lows. The highs tended to come in the spring and fall, the lows in winter and summer.

Those periods match the traditional seasons of the sport, at least in the United States. Before year-round road racing grew up in this country, before there were winter indoor track meets and the outdoor season had spread into summer, we ran track from about March to May and cross-country from September to November. We ran easily, if at all, between racing seasons.

We now can race as often as every few days and can continue racing this way year-round. But you shouldn't yield to that temptation.

No one would want to return to those bad old days when we had no choice but to limit our racing. The *chance* to race year-round has been a wonderful advance. But it puts the responsibility on us to choose carefully when we'll race and when we'll abstain.

The racing opportunities have improved, but the rules haven't changed. It's still a very rare runner who can race well indefinitely.

The year still needs a focus, a peak period. It also still needs a rebuilding phase.

Tom Osler's practice of matching the highs and lows of racing to the seasons of the year makes good sense. The best weather and most of the best races occur in spring and fall, and the least attractive racing comes in the coldest and hottest months. Racing energies ebb and flow with the seasons, so schedule your year to take advantage of the calendar's natural ups and downs.

In the timeless words of Ecclesiastes, there is "a time to sow and a time to reap, a time to break down and a time to build up." Schedule seasons both high and low—seasons for sowing with slower and easier running, and seasons for reaping with hard training and racing.

CHAPTER 6

Endure the Roadblocks to Success

Toughness is running around and through obstacles that stand between you and your goals.

—The Self-Inflicted Suffering—

Unfortunately, training and racing are not perfectly safe. They are hard work, and can easily cross the line into *overwork*. The injury rate in this seemingly nonviolent sport is high. In any year, for example, one runner in every two is hurt badly enough to require a layoff, medical treatment, or both. Most of these injuries are self-inflicted. They result neither from a competitor's blows (as might happen in football) nor random accidents (such as hitting a hidden rock while skiing). The stress of running itself takes the blame in a high percentage of cases.

Certain illnesses such as the cold also can be self-inflicted. You're constantly exposed to a variety of common illnesses, yet they rarely take hold unless stress has broken down the body's natural defenses. In that sense, you don't so much catch a cold as it catches *you*.

The great majority of medical conditions that slow or stop runners grow out of what the sports doctors call "overuse": too much wear and tear on a body not conditioned to handle so much stress. In this fact lies hope. Because you cause most of your own ailments, you can also prevent them. Most running ailments aren't punishment inflicted by the wrathful gods: they are the predictable result of too much work and too little attention paid to obvious warnings. You hold the power to avoid this type of trouble.

If you apply stress in small, regular doses, the body adapts to it by growing stronger. But if the doses are too heavy, the body can't cope. It slips into the "exhaustion" phase and becomes susceptible to physical breakdown. The trick in training, then, is to run hard enough to build but not so hard that you tear down. The same type of activity can either help or hurt, depending on its dosage.

How do you determine the right amount? Adaptive success and failure are fairly easy to detect. Improved performance accompanied by injury- and illness-free activity indicates that you're adapting nicely to this stress. However, when the stress load grows too heavy—for whatever reason—certain mild symptoms appear.

The symptoms listed below warn that more serious trouble might develop if you don't take immediate preventive action. Develop a sensitivity to these signals. By quickly reading, interpreting, and acting upon them, you can usually stop trouble at its source.

Prevention of injuries and illnesses involves reducing or eliminating stresses. One of the most flexible stresses is your training load. Adjust it whenever you notice any of the warnings described in the next section.

—The Symptoms of Overworking—

Eugene, Oregon, bills itself as the nation's "running capital." And who can argue with that claim? Eugene is home to the University of Oregon, whose track and cross-country teams consistently rank among the NCAA leaders. Many of the country's best-known runners, including Mary Decker Slaney and Alberto Salazar, live in Eugene.

Because elite athletes in peak condition stand on the brink of injury and illness, Eugene also has grown into a sports medicine center. Dick Brown has played many roles in this network—notably as Decker Slaney's coach during her longest injury-free period (1981–84) and time of greatest competitive success (two World Championships in 1983), and as a physiology researcher for Athletics West track club. Brown's studies in Eugene included an attempt to provide runners with simple guidelines for determining when they were training and when they were straining. He says, "We've all heard the admonition, 'Listen to your body.' But many runners don't know what messages to listen for, or how to respond to them."

Brown listed 30 potential stress indicators. Then he measured these for 10 top-level runners over a 10-month period, correlating the results with their levels of health and performance. These tests showed that 13 of the factors were statistically significant indicators of overstress. Three of them stood out as the clearest warnings. Brown says, "Our research showed that these three indicators have the potential to serve as general guidance tools for most athletes. They are hours slept, morning pulse rate, and morning body weight."

Brown's guidelines for using the critical figures:

1. "Measure, record, and maintain a running average of your hours slept, morning pulse rate, and morning body weight. The hours slept should be as close an estimate as possible of when you fell asleep until you woke up. The one-minute morning pulse should be taken before getting out of bed. The morning body weight should be taken after voiding and prior to any food intake."

You're Tough Enough If. . .

▲ *You realize that most running ailments are self-inflicted.*
▲ *You read the warnings telling you how much running is too much.*
▲ *You heed minor symptoms before they grow into major problems.*
▲ *You substitute whatever activity doesn't make the problem worse.*
▲ *You admit there are days when resting helps more than working.*
▲ *You recognize that a breakdown is a way to get a needed break.*
▲ *You realize that time off is the best cure for these ailments.*
▲ *You take very seriously the main threat to road runners: drivers.*
▲ *You adjust to the many imperfections of weather conditions.*
▲ *You adapt to a wide variety of running surfaces and shoes.*

---

2. "Compare each day's data with your averages by asking: 'Did I sleep 10 percent less than normal?' 'Was my morning pulse 10 percent higher than normal?' 'Did I weigh three percent less than normal?' "

3. "If you get one 'yes' answer, plan to cut back your training load if you are having trouble during the day's workout. If you get two 'yes' answers, plan to have an easy workout that day. If you get three 'yes' answers, your body is telling you it needs more recovery time and you should consider taking the day off. Taking one day off promptly may prevent taking lots of days off later."

Dick Brown cites two examples of Athletics West runners who benefited from these stress indicators. Ken Martin was training for a steeplechase race when he complained of being extremely tired. His weight had dropped into the danger zone. Brown says, "Ken was advised to discontinue any training until race day. By then, his weight was back to normal, and he ran his personal-best time. Temporarily reducing the stressors gave his body a chance to recover."

One winter, Mary Decker Slaney set a world outoor record for the mile in New Zealand. She immediately launched a successful indoor season in the United States but was feeling tired before it ended. "Officials from the National Indoor Championships still wanted her to compete there," says Brown. "Mary knew her racing was over for the winter but was having a hard time saying 'no' to this invitation." Like Ken Martin, Mary's weight had fallen significantly below her norm. A skinfold measurement for body fat and a blood test gave supporting evidence that she was run down. "Armed with this information," Brown recalls, "she could say 'no' firmly and without any feeling of guilt for not fulfilling a request."

We all sometimes need good, guilt-free reasons to say "no" to ourselves.

—The Toll Running Takes—

Injuries can be good for us. Without them, we runners would have to find a new topic to start our conversations. Without injuries forcing us to take needed breaks from

For Steve Prefontaine (United States), toughness meant taking charge of a race, setting both its pace and style. He wasn't just a runner: he was a performer whose loss is still felt long after his death in a 1975 auto accident.

training and racing, we wouldn't ever stop voluntarily. Injury-free running is not only unlikely but also perhaps undesirable.

The only way to stamp out injuries is to stop running completely, which is unthinkable. The surest way to limit injuries is to avoid the racing and training that make running worth doing.

Whenever runners push our limits for distance or pace, we also go to the brink of injury. One of the great attractions of the running sport (as opposed to the exercise) is seeing how far we can bend without breaking.

We often break. Surveys taken by *Runner's World* magazine report that at least every other reader will be hurt in any year. The casualty figure stood at 56 percent in a late-1980s poll, down by about 10 percent from the count a decade earlier. This drop suggests that runners as a group do slightly better now at bending without breaking. But the fact remains that only a minority of runners escape unhurt in any one year, and almost no one does over a career.

The statistics sound worse than they are, because they don't define "injury." Runners rarely get hurt seriously or permanently. Our injuries don't fall into the same class as career-ending football knees or baseball shoulders. To a runner, an injury is any problem bad enough to disrupt the normal flow of running. Minor damage will do that. A sore spot the size of a dime and the severity of a toothache can cripple a runner. The pain of not being able to run usually hurts worse than the injury itself, which may not hurt at all except when you try to run on it.

A study by Dr. John Pagliano involving thousands of runners in his podiatry practice indicates that their complaints are rarely serious and seldom permanent. Time heals nearly everything, as long as the root causes are eliminated or modified. Most running injuries result from preventable and correctable mistakes, not random accidents. "The number-one cause of injuries is a mistake in the training program," says noted sports orthopedist Dr. Stan James. "That accounts for almost two-thirds of the breakdowns. Obviously, then, the way to prevent most injuries is to avoid making these mistakes in training."

Experience teaches, and the worst experiences teach best. Dr. James learned the most about training mistakes by making his own during competitive running and cross-country skiing. "I've made all the mistakes," he says. "I know what it's like to feel tired all the time and have had a lot of injuries through the years."

His health, energy, and performance all improved dramatically after these problems forced him to rethink and revise his own program. James first had to stumble and fall before he fully realized why he'd tripped. That's the main benefit of injuries: they get your attention. You need one major injury as a powerful lesson in how to run and why you run.

You don't need to go looking for the Big One. If you run long enough and hard enough, it will likely find *you.* And when it does, when you can't run at all and wonder if you ever will again, that's when you see clearly what went wrong. That's when you swear to take a better course if/when you recover. That's when you find out how much running means to you, after almost losing it.

The only bad injuries are the ones you don't learn from and don't get over.

—The Recovery from Injury—

Success and pain go together, on opposite sides of a very thin line. Being in top shape is one small step away from being injured. And the only sure way to avoid injury is to settle for the ordinary.

Britons Sebastian Coe, Steve Cram, and Steve Ovett are extraordinary runners. All have set world records. All have hurt themselves a lot. All have been subjects of biographies. Reviewer Ed Fox of *Track & Field News* writes, "The common theme that strikes me in all these accounts is the regular oscillation between fitness and injury of the top-level runner. Each book spends considerable time on the athlete's frustration and his questionable future when sidelined by debilitating injury."

Few of us will ever know how it feels to break a record. But most of us know only too well the feeling of breaking down. When our little goals are put on hold, we know some of the frustration and fear that the best runners experience. The worst pain from an injury isn't physical. What hurts the most is not being able to run normally and having doubts about ever being able to do it again.

Let's say an injury has knocked you off your feet. What to do then? Whatever the specific problem is, the basic rule is the same: stay as active as possible to keep the demon of self-doubt at bay. Whatever the problem, the road back to health follows a similar path. It starts with some "don'ts":

- *Don't make a bad problem worse* by trying to train through pain. Attempt nothing that causes you to limp or "favor" the injured area.
- *Don't worry about losing fitness.* If you developed it over months and years, it won't disappear in days and weeks.
- *Don't take an all-or-nothing approach.* Instead of giving up your training routine completely if you can't handle all of it, mimic it with alternate or modified activity.

Choose a substitute exercise that doesn't aggravate the problem. Then train at the normal time of day and for the normal period of time to keep your regular habits alive. For instance, if you can't run steadily without limping, mix walking and running. If no running is possible, just walk. If walking hurts too much, bike or swim.

As recovery progresses, work up the exercise ladder by the following steps:

1. *Biking or swimming.* These activities relieve most of the pressure from foot and leg injuries, while still allowing steady training.
2. *Walking.* Start it as soon as you can move without favoring the injured limb, and continue as long as pain doesn't become intense. (These limitations apply at all stages.)
3. *Walking mixed with running.* As the walks become too easy, add brief periods of easy running—as little as one minute after each five minutes of walking at first. Gradually build up the amount of running—to, say, five minutes at a time with one-minute walks.
4. *Running again.* When you can tolerate a nonstop run, approach it cautiously. Keep the distances and paces modest at first.
5. *Returning to racing.* Add longer and faster training only when you can handle typical daily runs comfortably. Race again only after you've passed the tests of long runs and speed work.

A similar plan, minus stage one, can ease you back into training after a prolonged illness. Or it can work after a voluntary layoff during which your fitness has slipped badly.

Not all problems go away quickly. But most of them heal steadily and completely if treated right.

—The Treatment of Illness—

Running sometimes makes people ill—literally—but it also can act as preventive medicine or an aid to treatment. It all depends on how you use the running, or abuse it.

The good news first: evidence gleaned from several scientific studies indicates that runners, as a group, suffer fewer colds than nonexercisers. This apparently has to do with normal increases in body heat during activity that may destroy some of the "bugs."

However, continued hard work in the face of early symptoms can turn a mild cold into a dreadful one—and lead to such side effects as bronchitis. Coming down with a cold means you already have worked too hard.

Dr. George Sheehan, a sports medicine columnist for several magazines, spends a large part of each month counseling ailing athletes. Here is a summary of his advice for handling this most common of illnesses: "Treat a cold with respect. It is my feeling that it represents a breakdown in the defense system. The cold is an early warning of exhaustion." Dr. Sheehan says to heed your body's warnings, and to cut back or even cut out training for the first one to three days of a cold. "Then resume at a slow pace for relatively short distances." He recommends not waiting for all symptoms to subside. Moderate exercise in the waning stages of the illness, says Sheehan, helps clear away the lingering congestion.

Dr. Terry Kavanagh, a Canadian who pioneered the use of running for heart patients (including those receiving transplants), agrees that "if it's a common cold without a fever, mild exercise may shorten the duration of the cold." Dr. Sheehan also emphasizes, "Don't run with a fever. Rest until it passes. After that, as a rule of thumb, take two easy days for each day of fever. A week of fever, therefore, would need an additional two weeks' recovery period. Exhausting workouts should be avoided at this time, or recurrence of the illness is a distinct possibility."

This advice can't be stressed too strongly. Ignoring it can lead to severe complications, including heart problems.

Dr. David Bewick, a cardiac researcher from Canada, noticed that the flu temporarily affected the heart in nearly all of his test subjects. "Our findings suggest that cardiac involvement in the various viral syndromes may be tissue-specific," says Dr. Bewick, "with influenza affecting mainly the myocardium [a muscular layer of the heart wall]." Bewick adds that "our people were young and at the very mild end of the spectrum. When the viral infection subsided, their hearts got back to normal."

He warns against trying to "run off" the illness. An example of where that might lead comes from a high-level source. Steve Ovett, an Olympic track champion and former world record-holder, recalls what happened to him before, during, and long after the 1984 Olympic Games. "I had the flu," says the British runner. "But with the Games coming up, I trained through my illness and thought I was over it. In Los

Angeles, I knew something was wrong. The harder I pushed, the worse the pains in my chest got. I had all the classic symptoms of a heart attack, and finally my body just quit."

Ovett dropped out of the 1500-meter final. But his problems were far from over. "It wasn't until after the Games," he recalls, "that I learned I had pericarditis—a viral infection of the sac covering the heart. It took me five months to recover fully."

Dr. Terry Kavanagh advises, "If you have a fever, usually associated with the flu, stop all exercise. The body can't cope with the double stress. I tell people to wait until they are fully recovered from the flu and then to add five days before they begin running again."

Exhaustion led, at least in part, to contracting this illness. Therefore, avoiding further exhausting efforts is your best medicine.

—The Rules of Roads—

Dr. George Sheehan once remarked with tongue only partly in cheek that runners have three natural enemies: "dogs, drivers, and doctors." He explained that each group seems bent on taking away our activity. Dogs attack. Drivers rule the roads. And some doctors say, "If it hurts to run, then don't run."

Fortunately, the medical profession has come to realize that what runners want most is to keep running. Progressive doctors, many of them runners themselves, now provide solid information about avoiding and treating injuries rather than dispensing simplistic "stop-doing-it" advice. These onetime adversaries have been converted to friends. And yapping dogs, as well as the human hecklers who resemble yapping dogs, are more a nuisance than a threat.

My concern here centers on the remaining enemy: the driver. Drivers mean runners no harm, but the vehicles they steer can strike us with deadly force.

Streets and roads are convenient places to run, and you probably do most of your training there. They offer smooth, all-weather surfaces. In town, streets are lighted for safer night training. You hit the roads for their convenience, and in doing so court their dangers. Training in traffic is the greatest risk a runner faces.

The Insurance Institute for Highway Safety once analyzed 60 runner/auto collisions occurring during a one-year period. In each case, investigators assessed blame to the runner, driver, or both. But these questions are academic, particularly to the survivors of runners who died in about half these accidents. Most of the others suffered injuries that halted their running for a long time or permanently.

Look at the odds: you take 100 to 200 pounds of soft flesh to the road, and travel five to 10 miles an hour. The automobile weighs more than 10 times that much, can travel 10 times as fast, and is made of hard metal. Hundreds of cars may pass within a few feet of you on each run. If one driver veers just slightly the wrong way at the wrong moment, or if you do, you lose no matter who's to blame.

With those sobering facts in mind, study the following rules for road safety:

1. When training on the roads, always yield the right of way even when it's rightly yours. The roads *always* belong to the vehicles, if only because of their size and speed.
2. Run defensively and with a hint of paranoia. Assume that all drivers are out to get you, and don't give them that chance.
3. Stay awake. Fight the tendency to daydream the miles away. Keep your head up and your eyes on the road.
4. Be seen, especially when training in the darkness. Wear brightly colored clothing in the daytime and reflective items at night.
5. See what's coming. Wear a visor or billed cap in darkness to shade your eyes from headlights that could blind you because drivers rarely dim their lights for oncoming pedestrians.
6. Hear what's coming. Leave your cassette tape player or earphone radio at home where it won't drown out warnings of danger.
7. Be most careful at sunrise and sunset. Rush-hour traffic, sleepy or exhausted commuters, and the glare of the low sun in the drivers' or your eyes make these the most dangerous hours.
8. Use sidewalks whenever possible. If you must use the roadways, choose those with wide shoulders and preferably run on the left side, facing oncoming traffic.
9. Don't ignore bicycles and motorcycles. They travel almost as fast as cars on city streets, are less visible, and can inflict great damage both to you and their riders.
10. Don't provoke drivers by invading their lane, darting across in front of them, or berating them in cases of close calls. A car can be a deadly weapon in the hands of an angry driver.

—The Air Around You—

This is not a perfect world. The weather seldom is just right, and as a runner you must deal with whatever you're given. Learn to accept the fact that the weather won't adapt to you, so you must adapt to it. Adjust how much and how fast you run, where you run, and what you wear according to the conditions.

Maybe you can't run as much or as often as you'd like. But more often than not, you can do something—and anything is better than nothing. After all, maybe only one day a week is perfectly conducive to running. That single day does not a runner make.

When dealing with either heat or cold, recognize the difference between standing around in this weather and running in it. Heat intensifies when you run, and cold loses some of its sting, because the body is a great furnace but a poor air conditioner.

Heat

Running on a hot day increases the body's heat production. So a nice afternoon for suntanning beside the pool may be brutal for training.

For Jim Ryun (number 265, from the United States), toughness meant encountering the pressures of expectations that go with early fame. He set world mile records at 19 and 20, but was unfairly labeled a ''loser'' for lack of Olympic golds.

A 20-degree rule applies to running. The perceived temperature automatically rises by about that much in the course of a run. So a nice, sunny, 70-degree afternoon soon feels like a sizzling 90.

High humidity readings widen this gap, making hot days feel even hotter. The closer the air is to the saturation point, the slower your sweat evaporates and the less well the air cools you.

The body acts on what it feels, not on what the thermometer reads. As internal heat goes up, you compensate by sweating more and can only sweat so much before dehydration sets in. A three-percent loss of fluid weight affects performance. A six-percent deficit threatens health.

A pint of sweat weighs a pound. You may drain off a half-gallon or more during a hot-weather run. After a large sweat loss, it may take you a day or two to redress the balance. Chronic dehydration may result from repeated heavy drains and inadequate replacement.

The best way to gauge sweat debt is to check your prerun and postrun weights each day in hot weather. Drinking immediately before, during, and after running won't completely eliminate losses. But you can replace enough of the lost fluid to at least keep the running safe, if not productive.

Cold

The warming effect of running works to your benefit here. A chilling 30-degree day is transformed into a pleasant 50 during a run. A cold 10-degree morning rises to a tolerable 30.

Humidity makes summer weather unbearable. Wind makes winter weather especially painful. Each mile per hour of wind drops the apparent temperature by about one degree. As the windchill reading drops, the threat of frostbite climbs.

However, on typical winter days, there is little risk of frostbite if you keep moving and cover your hands and ears. As for fears of "freezing the lungs" by breathing the icy air, they're groundless. People ski, both downhill and cross-country, in winter. They ice-skate, ride snowmobiles, even sit and fish. Why not run?

Just dress for the conditions. But remember again to dress for a temperature that will seem 20 degrees warmer during the run than it felt at the start. Don't overdress and come home looking like a clothesline, draped with your castoffs.

Wind

Moving air is a mixed blessing. Sometimes it helps your running, and sometimes it hurts. A tail wind speeds you up, and a head wind slows you down. You know that. Less obvious is the fact that on a course with equal portions of wind in the face and at the back, the losses always outweigh the gains.

Tail winds make a hot day feel hotter by reducing the wind's cooling effect. Head winds make a cold day feel colder by creating a windchill.

Choose courses that take maximum advantage of wind direction. As much as possible, avoid head winds in winter but seek them out in summer.

If you must run an out-and-back course, save the best part for last. Return home with the chilling winds of winter behind you and the cooling breezes of summer in your face.

—The Earth Under You—

Surfaces

Runner's World once unmasked a myth, the one that says pounding along on hard surfaces increases the risk of injuries. The magazine surveyed thousands of runners. Those who trained on grass and dirt, which are thought to be the kindest surfaces on your feet and legs, reported that they got hurt just as often as those who ran entirely on asphalt and concrete. The conclusions from this poll: (1) modern supportive and shock-absorbing shoes have neutralized much of the pounding, and (2) errors in how a person runs—the routine itself—are more likely to cause problems than where a person runs.

Most runners now train on the roads, for reasons noted in chapter 5: you can run there at all hours and find sure, smooth footing in all weather conditions.

While practicalities dictate that much of your training will be on hard surfaces, don't deprive yourself completely of the softer ones. The study quoted above ignores one key fact: minor aches (as opposed to true injuries) clearly increase from the constant pounding of hard road surfaces, and the soft ones are more pleasing aesthetically.

Experience all the different kinds of surfaces. Mix runs on city streets and grassy fields, country roads and forest trails, concrete sidewalks and cinder or rubbery tracks. Get used to them all so no sudden change in surface will come as a shock.

Hills

Hills make for harder work, whether the surface is soft or unyielding. They send breathing rates to their peak, well past ideal aerobic training levels.

Both up and down, hills also work the legs in different ways than running on the flat does. Uphills increase the work load of the upper-leg muscles, while downhills increase the pounding stress on all the muscles, tendons, and joints.

Dr. David Costill, the sport's foremost physiologist, says, "Hilly terrain will significantly impair a runner's performance." His research indicates that even with an equal amount of climbing and descending, you use more energy and lose more time on hills compared with flat runs.

Give hills your respect. They shrink for no one, so you have to adapt to them. Adapt by changing your running form. Adjust to running in hills as you would while riding a multispeed bicycle on hilly terrain. You wouldn't ride up and down in the same gear used on the flat. You'd shift, pump, coast, and brake in tune with the slope—all the while maintaining a constant pedaling rate.

You, too, have many running gears. Shift into the lower ones while running uphill. Try to keep the *effort* fairly constant, which means reducing the pace. While going downhill, shift into a higher gear. You then go faster as the effort stays the same.

Shoes

There isn't room here for advice on which shoes to buy. Just remember to buy several pairs and rotate them, using different shoes for different surfaces and terrains or mixing them for the sake of mixing.

Rotate shoes to equalize the stresses that are slightly different for each model, and even with two pairs of the same model. This practice may keep injuries from creeping up on you.

Each model has its own quirks. The little stresses they cause can grow into big pains when repeated a thousand times per mile for days on end. Rotating shoes never allows one type of stress more than a day at a time to build up.

Put three or four widely varied pairs into your rotation. The cost may seem extravagant, but remember that each pair of shoes will now last three or four times longer than if you wore them constantly. Alternate the shoes from day to day, and drop any shoe from the rotation if it repeatedly causes problems.

—PART III—
RUNNING
THE RACE

—CHAPTER 7—

Accept Prerace Doubts and Fears

Toughness is weathering the worries that precede the excitement of racing.

—The Rituals of Racers—

Runners on the verge of racing act strangely. We worry about hangnails, stomachaches, and other minor problems that might prevent us from experiencing the real pains of the race.

The mind plays tricks as the race approaches. It magnifies trivia into critical concerns.

You can't wait to get started. And at the same time, you don't want to start—or don't know if you can.

The last hours drag unmercifully, and a troubled mind fills them with a month's worth of worry. Every move, every thought seems to pass under a microscope.

"I've got to get some sleep. How can I run if I can't keep my eyes open?"

"Should I eat this? It might upset my stomach."

"Oh no, my shorts are rubbing! Think what this will do to my legs after a couple of miles."

"My left shoe has a flaw. Will my feet survive unblistered?"

"Nausea. Could it be the flu?"

"Uh-oh, a twinge in my calf!"

"Is that the wind I hear? Is the temperature climbing?"

"Look how fit and relaxed all the other runners are."

Waiting for a race to start is like walking up a dark alley in a dangerous part of town, knowing you'll probably be mugged but not knowing exactly when or how. Jittery runners concoct odd rituals to help weather these preevent emotional storms.

Dick Beardsley used rituals while becoming one of the fastest U.S. marathoners in history. He admits to spitting twice on the starting line and then wiping away the spit with his foot. He admits to sliding his wedding ring off and on exactly four times within one minute of the start. But he worries that "the men in white coats will come and take me away if I tell this story." Then he goes ahead with the telling.

He insisted on racing in the same shoes, shorts, and singlet that served him well in his last good race. Trouble was, he ran so many good races one year that the lucky outfit had started to show wear. He fretted over his decision to abandon these items before his biggest race. Then at the last minute, he solved his dilemma. The Beardsleys were staying within sight of the finish line. As they left the hotel, Dick told his wife Mary, "Wait here. I'll be right back. I forgot something." He rushed into the room. There, he hung his clothes and set his shoes in the window. "If I couldn't wear them," he says, "then at least they could watch how I did." The old outfit must have approved. That day, it saw Beardsley run the second-best time ever for an American.

Rituals are neutral acts. They don't interfere with the race, or we would have dropped them the first time they cost us a few seconds. But rituals give little direct aid, either. This fact separates them from profitable moves like eating a proper prerace meal and taking a well-timed warm-up.

Rituals are safety valves for tension. They help keep worries from running out of control. They do more to psych us *down* than up before races.

Training already has set the upper limits of race performance. Once the training is in the bank, the goal shifts to reaching the starting line healthy, fresh, and eager to race. Prerace rituals, silly as they may seem, serve those ends. The main intent of ritualistic behavior is to settle the mind. You grasp onto things familiar before plunging into the unknown.

Planning the race serves the same purpose. You take comfort in having a general idea—based on past experiences—of what is going to happen, when, and how you'll react when it does. (Chapter 8 deals with specific race planning.)

But you can't know exactly what the race will hold, and probably wouldn't even want to know in advance. Exploring the unknown is as fascinating as it is frightening.

—The Symptoms of Uncertainty—

After setting a Boston Marathon course record in 1970, Ron Hill said, "I was worrying like hell all the way. But this is a good thing to develop, you know—this fear. It keeps you moving." Hill had long since come to grips with fear. He learned to recognize it as a fact of competitive life that could be channeled to work for him.

It hadn't always been that way. He recalled how fear had worked against him at the 1964 Olympics. "When I was in Tokyo," he said, "I was the second-fastest man in the world at 10,000 meters. But the night before the race, I was thinking, 'Tomorrow's the day!' There I was, lying in bed, turning the race over in my mind. And the first thing I thought about when I woke up was, 'Today's the day!' My stomach turned

---

You're Tough Enough If. . .

▲ *You train down (taper) for days or even weeks before racing.*
▲ *You fuel up (take extra carbohydrates) for the last few days before a race.*
▲ *You go into the race feeling healthy, energetic, and eager.*
▲ *You set race goals that give you a good chance of winning.*
▲ *You don't set goals so low that they make victories meaningless.*
▲ *You try no untested foods, drinks, clothes, or shoes on race day.*
▲ *You accept anxiety as necessary preparation for the hard work ahead.*
▲ *You adopt rituals to ease you through the prerace waiting period.*
▲ *You stay loose mentally by sitting down to relaxation exercises.*
▲ *You get loose physically with warming up for the racing ahead.*

---

over. I didn't want to get out of bed, but finally dragged myself out. During the warm-up, my legs felt like lead, and I was just dragging myself around the track during the race. There was no desire to get into the competition. In fact, the only desire was to get away from it. If somehow I could have gotten out of it, I wouldn't have run at all. I finished a disgusting 18th."

Hill immediately set about finding ways to cope with prerace anxiety. He succeeded to the extent that he won the Boston Marathon, won the Commonwealth Games and European Championships marathons, and set world records.

The fear remained, Hill admitted. But he learned to make it work *for* him instead of against him. He said, "The fear of running a long race can come from the fact that you know it's going to be physically painful. And unless you are a masochist, nobody likes pain. I certainly don't like it. If you dwell on the painful aspect, it can make you nervous. I've developed some ways that I can step outside myself. I talk about the race in terms of what it's going to involve physically, and where the pain is going to come, and what it's going to feel like, and how distressing it's going to be—without actually thinking that the guy who's speaking is going to be in that position so many hours hence."

Ron Hill learned some important lessons about prerace jitters that you also might find helpful. He realized that, within limits, his condition was normal and even beneficial. By knowing the signs and symptoms, and accepting them as natural, he was better able to control his anxiety.

Prerace fear takes many forms: fear of pain, fear of competitors, fear of failure, fear of fear itself. The fears arise in part from what scientists call "fight-or-flight reactions." These are the body's and mind's normal ways of preparing you for any potentially stressful encounter. They're only harmful when they reach such extremes that they interfere with your performance instead of enhancing it.

Anyone who has raced will recognize these physical/emotional reactions. The most telling signs in the last hours before racing are:

1. Interrupted sleep the night before, often including nightmares linked to the race
2. Queasy stomach, often accompanied by loss of appetite and sometimes vomiting

For Alberto Salazar (number 936, from the United States), toughness has meant dealing with both the rewards of hard work—a world marathon best at age 23 — and its toll. A series of illnesses and injuries have slowed him since 1983.

3. Frequent urination and symptoms of diarrhea
4. Muscle tension, particularly in the neck and shoulders
5. Feelings of drained energy
6. Magnified concern over minor aches and pains
7. Irritability with family and friends
8. Lack of concentration on anything but the event at hand
9. Desire to escape the event at hand
10. Need to make excuses in advance in case of failure

Whatever form it takes, a certain amount of uneasiness is a fact of the racer's life. It may feel unpleasant, but it isn't all bad. This is the mind's way of warming up the body for the big task ahead. Think of your fear as doing you a favor.

— The Last Days' Training —

Herbie Hamilton and Byron Moore faced their first marathon. The running partners from Louisiana had trained enough for the race and knew what to expect in it. But they didn't know what to do in the lull between the end of their hard training and the start of hard racing. "What should we do the last week before the marathon?" they asked an experienced marathoner. "We're new at this and would appreciate your experienced suggestions."

Hamilton and Moore were told that experienced runners get excited, too. They feel impatient and confused in the final days before races. They make mistakes. The main one is training too hard, too late. Runners act like nervous students cramming for final exams after letting their studies slide all semester. The main advice to Hamilton and Moore was, "Don't train that week. At least don't do anything that takes much effort."

Hard work won't help now. Training has a delayed-reaction effect, meaning that you don't get stronger and faster tomorrow by working hard today. You race on training done last week, last month, even last year.

Training benefits add up slowly. You can't cram the last few days with all the work you can stand, expecting to make up for what you skipped earlier. But it is never too late to tire or hurt yourself so much that you negate the good training you've stored away.

Do the last long or fast training at least a week before a big race. Then let yourself be lazy. Short, easy runs are the only kind that can help you this late.

Total rest might help more, but few of us will allow ourselves such total rest. We keep running in the final days for the mind, not the body—to keep from thinking we've forgotten how to run.

No one speaks with more authority about proper tapering than Dr. David Costill. He knows the subject as an eminent sports physiologist and as a practicing athlete. As noted in chapter 5, Dr. Costill gave up running in the early 1980s. He went back to a sport, swimming, that he'd practiced decades earlier. "I had quit swimming after competing at Ohio University," he says, "because that was what swimmers did then: retire early."

Then came the injuries to both knees from running. Costill returned to the pool, his old swim skills came back, and soon he was racing again. Not only was he competing, but he was doing better than he ever had in college. Not only better against men his own age, but better against the clock because his training has improved.

He says, "I've been able to put to use some of the practical lessons learned from running and the laboratory." He now trains less than his competitors and rests more, because he knows better when to build up and when to taper off. "A final major factor in my second life as a swimmer," says Costill, "is that I've learned a lot over the years about how to rest up for competition. In swimming, you can taper for up to three weeks by just warming up every day."

What difference does this make? "If I try to compete now without tapering this way, then the times are almost identical to what I swam in college." In other words, they aren't as good as they could be.

—The Last Days' Eating—

This is not advice about how to eat right for long-term health. This is a brief summary of what happens when a runner eats wrong before a race and suffers for his mistake during the race.

In terms of general health, you are what you eat. But your running performance is just as closely linked to what you *don't* eat.

The most visible result of overeating is, of course, excess weight that you must pick up and carry with each step. But that, too, is a subject for other books.

My concern here is with what can go wrong soon after your last meal. Such problems fall into two main categories: (1) eating too much, too close to race time, and (2) eating the wrong food at the wrong time.

Too Much, Too Late

We run best on an empty or nearly empty stomach. Arthur Lydiard, the coach from New Zealand, says that he rarely sees runners "collapse from malnutrition" while competing. But he often observes problems of the opposite type: runners doubling over from cramps, making pit stops, or complaining of unpleasant sloshing or bloated feelings.

Sugary foods and drinks also can play tricks on you. George Sheehan, the runners' doctor, recalls once taking a sweet drink about an hour before a long training run and almost fainting during that run. Dr. Sheehan realized later that he'd suffered "reactive hypoglycemia." The drink had triggered a quick rise in his blood sugar, the sugar level had peaked during the hour's wait, and then had plunged before the run started.

Eat lightly, if at all, in the last few hours before racing. If you drink in those hours, make it water.

Wrong Food, Wrong Time

Certain people react badly, and sometimes even violently, to certain food groups. Surprisingly, according to Dr. George Sheehan, two chief culprits may be the "perfect food" and the "staff of life." Dr. Sheehan notes that a great number of pleas for help come to him from runners who don't tolerate milk and bread products very well.

He describes symptoms in one of his patients, a talented long-distance runner named Gary. "Every time he had a tough race or workout, he came down with severe stomach pains. Sometimes he would have diarrhea and blood in his stools as well. When not running and at other times, he had few or no complaints."

When Gary first sought help from a different doctor, he was told nothing was abnormal. His difficulties stemmed from "too much stress during a race and too much nervousness anticipating it." Gary already knew that. But telling a distance runner to avoid stress is like telling a swimmer not to get wet.

Dr. Sheehan suspected a dietary cause. When Gary reduced his prerun meal to bread and still had trouble, they found their answer. He couldn't tolerate the gluten in wheat—and most other grains—before a workout or race.

"If you have symptoms presumably due to nerves or stress or hypoglycemia," advises Sheehan, "or if your arthritis or migraine or other chronic disease seems worse than it should be, think 'food intolerance.' " Then scout out a dietary cause for your complaints. Do this by adding or excluding suspect items, and by noting the reactions in a food diary.

"Some foods are seldom eaten, but when consumed cause violent symptoms," says Sheehan. "Common examples are lobster, crab, chocolate, nuts, and seasonal fruits." However, with runners "the problem most often arises from staples like milk, eggs, wheat, coffee, or tea. Almost always, the source is consumed daily."

He recommends going on an "exclusion diet" to find the culprit. "One method is to limit intake for one week to a single meat, a single fruit, and water. If symptoms are relieved, reintroduce one food each week to see which one provokes symptoms."

A basic rule for the prerace meal, both for timing and substance: err on the side of too soon rather than too late, and too little rather than too much. When in doubt about an item, don't eat it.

—The Last Few Hours—

You wake up, stand on the leading edge of the day, and tell yourself it is a day like any other: 24 hours long, with the same sunrise and sunset as always. You think, "A billion Chinese don't care what I do today." You say these things to calm yourself. But it doesn't work. You know and you care that today is The Day. *Race day.* Day of mystery, of anticipation, of dread.

Weeks or months ago, you made yourself a promise about this day. You counted down the days as you prepared for this one. You'll bore your family and friends with stories of what you did today. But what will you do today? You can't know until you race, so you wait... and wonder... and worry.

Worry leads to confusion, confusion to mistakes. To avoid making them, you need a plan. Draw it up before the big day arrives, and keep it simple enough to follow automatically in the final hours—a time when you aren't sure you can remember how to tie your shoes.

1. *Get up early.* You may jump right from bed into a run on other days, but don't try to race that way. You may risk injury by racing while stiff or sore, and you surely will lose time.

   Most road races start in the morning—some very early—so get up several hours earlier, even if it means beating the dawn. Take a walk in the fresh air to wake up and loosen up. Perhaps take a shower for the same reasons.

2. *Stay close to the bathroom.* Your plumbing is twice as busy as usual. This extra activity is a natural part of race day, so don't worry about the amount. Just make sure you don't carry to the starting line anything that might want out as you race.

3. *Eating is optional.* Do whatever you normally do. If you typically run in the morning, eight to 12 hours or more after your last meal, race that way.

   If you're used to eating before running, take what you know you can tolerate. Realize, though, that all you're doing is filling an empty spot, not getting much new energy this late.

4. *Drinking is essential.* Even on cool days, racers throw off liquids at an alarming rate. This starts before the race (for reasons given in Point 2).

   Don't give the inevitable fluid losses a head start. Drink your way to the starting line, making sure you replace much of what your nerves are flushing out. Take small amounts, often.

5. *Remember shoes and shorts.* The essential items are the easiest ones to forget when packing for a race. Put on your shorts and shoes at home so you'll know you have them.

6. *Arrive early.* If you must travel more than an hour on race day, allow extra time after your arrival to shake out the kinks of the trip.

7. *Sign up first.* Check in before you start to warm up. Pick a time when crowds are small, get in the shortest line, do your business, then hurry away to a quieter place.

8. *Avoid crowds.* Part of warming up for a race is simply thinking about it. You think best alone.

   Even if you don't want to be a loner, other runners might. Respect their privacy, and save most of the talking for after the race.

9. *Check the course.* Race day is too late for a complete tour. Your confidence is shaky enough without exposing it to every mile and hill. Distances seem twice as long and climbs twice as steep now as they will when you race them, so save those experiences for later.

   Just know where the starting line is, and if the finish is somewhere else. Find out exactly how you come in at the end, when fatigue may confuse you. Ask where the time checkpoints and aid stations will be.

10. *Embrace fear.* A little bit of it is good for you. It gets the adrenaline pumping, and that will allow you to race faster than you could while perfectly calm.

—The Way to Relax—

Relaxation doesn't come easily to hard-driving, goal-oriented runners—the ones known to carry a "Type-A personality." We work hard at the sport, but also need to work more at relaxing.

Runners who race have highly developed fight-or-flight responses, nature's way of preparing us to face danger or flee from it. But we are less skilled at turning off the stress left behind by excessive fight/flight reactions.

Easy running can be relaxing, but racing isn't. It can exaggerate tensions in an already chronically tense person. Unrelieved tension works at cross-purposes before a race by being physically draining and mentally distracting.

Dr. Herbert Benson says that "our society has given very little attention to the importance of relaxation. Perhaps our work ethic views a person who takes time off as 'unproductive' or 'lazy.' " Dr. Benson observed the effects of chronic tension while studying the causes and treatment of high blood pressure at Harvard Medical School. He later prescribed a nonmedical antidote called "The Relaxation Response." In a book by the same name, Benson simplified, demystified, and scientifically validated ancient techniques of meditation. He explains that his technique "is drawn with little embellishment from four basic components found in a myriad of historical methods. We claim no innovation but simply a scientific validation of age-old wisdom."

Those four elements are:

1. *A quiet setting.* "Ideally, you should choose an environment with as few distractions as possible," says Benson. "A quiet room is suitable, as is a place of worship. The quiet environment makes it easier to eliminate distracting thoughts."

2. *A mental focus.* Benson notes that "to shift the mind from logical, externally oriented thought, there should be a constant stimulus: a sound, word, or phrase repeated silently or aloud, or the fixed gazing at an object. Since one of the major difficulties in the elicitation of the Relaxation Response is 'mind-wandering,' the repetition of the word or phrase is a way to help break the train of distracting thoughts."

3. *A passive mind.* Benson calls this "perhaps the most important element in eliciting the Relaxation Response. Distracting thoughts will occur, but do not worry about them. When these thoughts do present themselves and you become aware of them, simply return to the repetition of the mental device."

4. *A comfortable position.* "Choose one that will allow you to remain in the same position for at least 20 minutes," advises Benson. "Usually a sitting position is recommended, because it keeps you from falling asleep. The desired state of consciousness is not sleep, but the same four elements will lead to sleep if you are lying down."

Prerace tension usually doesn't peak at the starting line, but before you start to warm up and release some of the growing pressure. It builds to its highest point when the body is idle but the imagination is most active.

If tension threatens to overwhelm you as race time approaches, let Dr. Herbert Benson guide you through the stages of his Relaxation Response:

"Sit quietly. Close your eyes. Deeply relax all your muscles, beginning at your feet and progressing up to your face. Keep them relaxed.

For Joan Benoit Samuelson (United States), toughness meant coming back from knee surgery to win the Olympic Marathon Trial 17 days later. Toughness meant running away from the Olympic field as if this were her private time trial.

"Breathe through your nose. Become aware of your breathing. As you breathe out, say the word 'one' silently to yourself. Breathe easily and naturally.

"Continue for 10 to 20 minutes. When you finish, sit quietly for several minutes, at first with your eyes closed and later with them open. Do not stand up for a few minutes."

If nothing else, those minutes of meditation speed up the wait for the running to begin.

—The Warm-up and the Cool-down—

Recall how you feel as you take your first steps each day. You're stiff, heavy, uncoordinated. Is this how you want to start a race?

Now recall how you feel after 15 minutes have passed. Sweat is flowing as freely as your strides. The running has taken control of itself, and you're on automatic pilot. This is how you want to feel at the start of a race.

Spend 15 minutes running easily to warm up. This is long enough to loosen you up, but not so long that you squander the energy reserves needed later.

Recognize the need to warm up for races of all distances and paces. But vary the routine as working conditions change.

How you vary it depends on the racing distance. The shorter and faster the event, the more you must run before it starts. The longer it is, the less preliminary running you need.

When racing at short distances (say, 10-K and less), add two more elements after the easy run: a set of stretching exercises, and striding at the pace of the race. Before a one-mile race, for instance, take the easy run and perhaps extend it beyond a quarter-hour. Then stop for a few minutes to walk and stretch. Finally, accelerate to top racing speed for about 100 meters and repeat three to five times.

Being too tired to run the distance is not a problem here. Being too *tight* to run it fast is the problem you're trying to correct in the warm-up.

Shorten the warm-up as the racing distance grows. Make stretching and striding optional.

If your objective is just to cover the distance and not to run it fast, simply warm up during the early miles of the race as you would on a daily run. In a marathon, for instance, take your first running step of the day at the gun. Starting cool helps you resist the urge to start too fast.

Overeager runners typically err on the side of excessive warm-up. You see them pounding the streets up to an hour before a 10-K race. This amount of prerace warming serves no physical purpose. It is merely an anxiety reaction.

Think of how you feel after a normal day's 30- to 60-minute run. Do you want to *start* your hard work feeling that way?

The same runners who warm up too much before a race are as likely to cool down too little afterward. You see them crossing the finish line, stumbling to a grassy area nearby, and immediately starting the postevent celebration. This is no way to start recovering. If the warm-up shifts gears between resting and hard work, the cool-down period is a necessary shift from racing back to resting.

Continued mild activity gradually slows down the racing metabolism, and also acts as a massage that gently works out the soreness and fatigue products generated by the earlier effort.

The pattern and pace of recovery are set in the first few minutes after a race ends. So keep moving. Walk for at least 15 minutes.

Yes, *walk*. Some experts advise you to run easily. But walking will give the same benefits with much less effort, and you already have worked hard enough.

Jack Rockett, a physician and veteran racer from Tennessee, values his postrace walking. "I've found that a walk at the end of a race keeps me from being so tight," he says. "If I walk a mile or two the same day I run a race, I am less sore in the following days."

Tom Osler agrees. The author of *The Serious Runner's Handbook* says that "brisk walking is an excellent start on the road to recovery." Osler recommends a brief walk immediately after finishing any race, then another stroll later in the day. "The worst thing you can do," he says, "is to stop immediately upon crossing the finish line and stand around talking to friends."

The talking can wait. The cool-down can't.

═CHAPTER 8═

Race at Your Best Pace

Toughness is resisting the urges to start too quickly and to finish too slowly.

─The Goal You Choose─

You have to challenge yourself. "All things considered," says sports psychologist Bruce Ogilvie, "outstanding athletes are at their very best when the odds are slightly against them. Ambitious people derive slight joy, if any, when their ability remains uncontested."

Challenge, yes. But the challenge must be within our reach.

Dr. Ogilvie and his colleague Dr. Thomas Tutko have written that "the level of aspiration must be slightly elevated so [athletes] are always striving or reaching—standing on their tiptoes, not off-balance or in fear of stumbling, but with a ready capacity to regain their balance should they have overreached their capacity."

How far can you stretch without falling? That's for you to learn.

Frank Shorter, the 1972 Olympic Marathon champion, says that high-level success wasn't what he set out to achieve. It sort of crept up on him. "If it doesn't, you're going to go through a lot of frustration," says Shorter. "Wanting to be the best in the world when you're a nine- or 10-minute two-miler [as Shorter was through much of his college career] isn't going to do you any good."

Adds Jack Bacheler, Shorter's Olympic teammate in 1972, "You have to keep a perspective about your goals. I've never been very goal-oriented, I guess. I remember starting out, I just wanted to make the high school varsity team. After that, I just wanted to run against this guy I didn't like, who happened to be the third man on the team. After beating him, I thought—gee, by the state meet it would be kind of neat to be first man. And after that—gee, I wonder if it would be possible to run in college." And on it went, step by step, until Bacheler placed ninth in the Olympic Marathon at Munich.

Gerry Lindgren wouldn't agree with this approach. Lindgren, a boy wonder of U.S. distance running, made the 1964 Olympic team as a high schooler. He belonged to the You-Can-Do-Anything school of thinking. He recognized no limits, physical or mental.

It wasn't always that way. When his coach told Lindgren that he could be the best high school runner in Spokane history, the compliment overwhelmed him. Gerry later adopted an approach to positive thinking that many runners could copy in part. But his method of achieving his high aims shouldn't attract many imitators. "There is a universal law in farming," Lindgren once said. "You can't plant corn and expect beans to come up. There is also a universal law of the mind. You can't plant negative thoughts and expect positive results to come out. Negative results will come back to you sooner or later. You have to be very positive. The more positive you are, the more you can do. I have very carefully planted the positive and weeded out the negative in my thinking."

Yes, but part of positive thinking is recognizing legitimate limits. This, Lindgren steadfastly refused to do late in his career. During the pre-Olympic winter of 1971-72, his training load approached 50 miles a day. "Maybe it isn't necessary to run 50 a day," he said then. "Someone may be able to win running less than that. I know that everyone I run against isn't going to be running 50 miles a day. But I can and will, and more than anything else I think it's going to help me. It's going to help my self-image. When I get on the track, I'll know I've done more than anyone else out there, and I'll know I'm stronger." But Gerry Lindgren never raced well again. A reality of the sport is that the runner who aims the highest and works the hardest doesn't always race the best.

—The Tactics of Racing—

In perhaps no other sport are the results more predictable before the event starts than in running. Training done in advance determines within a narrow range just how the race will go for each of its runners.

Racing isn't a gamble. You're almost certain to succeed if you prepare well, and you're equally likely to fail if you don't.

With the big race a week or so away, your performance limits are basically set. The training is in the bank, and you can't do much more to improve it. You race on deposits made weeks earlier, not those from these last days. If you must put in extra effort now, make it mental. Think about ways to make the most of your trained-in abilities.

One way is planning to stick with the practices that brought you this far. Wear no new shoes or new clothes in the race. Try no new foods or drinks in the final meal. The time for experimenting is the training period, not race day.

In the race, your most pressing tactical concern isn't to beat someone but to beat the clock. You must maneuver through a crowd to do that. Hundreds or even thousands

---

You're Tough Enough If. . .

▲ *You race mainly to beat your old PRs, not the other people.*
▲ *You pace the race so it will yield your best possible time.*
▲ *You spread your energy evenly over the full race distance.*
▲ *You forecast the time and plan your pace from past race results.*
▲ *You view the race as two parts—equal in speed, opposite in style.*
▲ *You run the first half with caution, the last half with abandon.*
▲ *You resist the temptation to go too fast in the first half.*
▲ *You wave the overeager starters good-bye and run your own pace.*
▲ *You fight the urge to slow down too much in the last half.*
▲ *You pass the people who started too fast and slowed too much.*

---

of runners pack the starting line. This inevitably leads to congestion and a slow beginning of the race. Reduce both frustration and lost seconds by timing yourself. Don't start your watch with the gun but when you begin running, which could be a minute or more later. You shouldn't penalize yourself for the time spent standing.

Once underway, keep your head while runners around you are losing theirs. Regardless of the distance, start cautiously. Hold back as they surge past you. Let them go. You'll see most of them again later, when you're pushing the pace and doing the passing that matters.

Any race you finish strongly is a good one. It rewards the work well done and inspires more of the same.

A race doesn't finish at the finish line but stays with you long after that day's running ends. Don't rush away from the finish line and miss the celebration. You can always run far and fast by yourself, but only at races can you share the experience with so many people who know what it all means. Stick around and swap war stories. Start your carbohydrate reloading by indulging in your favorite beverage with family and friends. Plan a meal with some of them later on, knowing that then you can eat anything you crave and in whatever amounts you want it.

Stay for the awards ceremony, and take inspiration from the people who are the best at what you do. Their feats don't diminish yours. Other runners may have gone faster than you this day, but no one could have run your race for you. Look at the numbers frozen on the face of your digital stopwatch as you finished, and be proud of them. You alone put them there.

Begin training again with essential repair work by allowing at least one easy day for each hard mile of racing, then commit yourself to a new race and train for it.

In this sense, the racing never stops. You're always training for a race, running it, or recovering from it. One event leads directly to the next and then the one after that. This is as it should be. The benefits of this sport have a short shelf life. Stop running, and they disappear almost immediately.

Racing has little to do directly with fitness. But its indirect contribution, as motivator to keep you doing the gentler running that does make you fit, is enormous.

For Frank Shorter (United States) toughness meant winning races — including the Olympic Marathon — without feeling the need to destroy an opponent. He sometimes intentionally tied with a teammate at the end of a hard-fought race.

— The Records You Set —

Runners who enter races come in two types, Racers and Pacers. Which one you are depends on your ability and personality. Racers run to beat other runners. They rank themselves against everyone in the race or in their division of it, and can't win without beating them all. This fact makes Racers such a small minority in any race field that I'll pay them little attention in this chapter. Pacers run to beat the clock. They rate themselves against their own times, and can win without beating anyone. The great majority of race entrants qualify as Pacers, so I'll focus here on their needs.

I'll talk mostly about the tactics needed to win by the watch. I'll talk about the tactics for collecting the Pacer's greatest reward: the PR. To a runner, PR doesn't stand for public relations or an island in the Caribbean. It means "personal record."

Traditionally, this sport picked its winners as all other sports do. The first person to finish won, and everyone else lost. The winner—and only that winner—could enhance this performance by setting a meet, state, national, or world record. But the invention of the digital stopwatch worn on the wrist turned everyone into a potential winner. This watch gave us a personal, accurate, and objective way to measure success and progress.

The digital watch also created the Pacer. Suddenly, winning didn't depend on beating anyone. We now judged winning by how our new numbers on the watch compared with old ones.

Be proud of your PRs, but not so proud that you want to preserve them. Your records, like all records, are made to be broken. No one can break them for you, and no one else can take them from you.

For the Pacer, a time is the only race prize that really means anything. Certificates and T-shirts go to anyone who pays an entry fee, but times must be earned. They don't come to you automatically, but must be won in a race against yourself.

You win the race against time and set records the way all athletes do: by preparing better than your opponent (in this case, your old self) and then racing smarter.

You've done the training. Now what can you add to your bag of tactical tricks that will shave extra seconds or minutes from the face of that digital watch?

1. *Pick your spots.* Race most seriously in the spring and fall, when the weather is likely to be most favorable for fast times. Choose a fast course (flat, perhaps, but not downhill; you don't want a phony PR) designated "certified" (meaning it has passed strict measurement tests and is certain not to be short).
2. *Avoid crowds.* For record attempts, find a race numbering 100 or fewer runners per kilometer (maximum of 1000 in a 10-K, up to about 4000 in a marathon) so they'll have room to spread out. Massive races are human traffic jams that cost you valuable time, while smaller events allow you to start running at the gun and to follow the straightest—shortest—possible course to the finish.
3. *Cut corners.* Don't run as if you were driving, always staying in the right-hand lane and making proper turns. Race courses are measured along the shortest possible route that you can travel, and you penalize yourself by straying from that path.
4. *Compete.* Realize that your placing as a Pacer ultimately means little, but still use the people in front of you as moving targets. After the starting rush is over and runners up

ahead have settled into their pace, reel them in one at a time. This tactic helps you without hurting them.

5. *Pace yourself.* Runners hit The Wall because they make one of two mistakes: training inadequately or pacing improperly. I'm assuming you've trained well, so this chapter deals with avoiding the second problem.

—The Forecast of Time—

Before you plan how to run a faster race, think how much faster you can run. "Set realistic goals," the sports psychologists tell you (see chapter 7). The quickest way to discourage yourself is to choose a target you can never hit. But what is "realistic"? What do recent times at one distance tell you about your potential results at a different distance?

There are ways to peer into your future. Graphs and formulas tell how to predict times ahead based on times past, from one distance to another. But be warned: the math can get a little complicated.

One rule of thumb is to add 20 seconds per mile to your predicted pace each time you double your racing distance. The difference in world-record pace—1500 to 3000 meters, 5000 to 10,000, 10-K to 20-K or half-marathon, and half- to full marathon— averages 17 seconds for the fastest and most durable athletes. For the rest of us, the 20-second rule of thumb may indeed apply.

Another formula: the pace typically slows by about 5 percent as the distance doubles, and improves by that amount as the distance drops by half. For instance, a half-marathon is roughly twice the length of a 10-K. Say you run the shorter distance at 6:30 mile pace. Add 5 percent to that (390 seconds times .05 equals 20 seconds), and you can count on running 6:50 miles during your half-marathon.

The formula has value even greater than predicting future results. It helps you plan races.

You can't know in advance exactly how any race will end, but the 5-percent formula can give you a better idea how it should *start.* Base your pacing plans on the predicted time.

Looking at the formula another way, you should expect about a five-minute improvement in marathon time and 2½ minutes in the half-marathon for each one-minute drop in 10-K time. This assumes, of course, that you are equally well trained for these distances.

Running writer Mike Tymn offers yet another formula for predicting times at the two most popular road racing distances, the 10-K and marathon. "Although the marathon is 4.22 times as long as the 10-K," says Tymn, "the average difference between the times of well-conditioned runners is 4.65." To calculate probable marathon time, multiply your most recent 10-K mark by 4.65. Someone capable of running a 40-minute 10-K should be able to do a 3:06 marathon (40 minutes times 4.65 equals 186 minutes).

Tymn notes that "you can divide your marathon time by 4.65 to predict your 10-K potential." A three-hour (180 minutes) marathoner should be able to run 38:42 (180 divided by 4.65 equals 38.7) if equally well trained for endurance and speed.

Your speed-up/slow-down factor probably won't be as exact as I've made them sound here. However, dramatic variations from these figures may signal the need for changes in training. A runner with highly polished speed but limited endurance will slow down more than normal as the distance increases. One who puts in megamiles of low quality will speed up less than normal as the distance drops. If you see less than the expected difference between 10-K and marathon pace, your speed needs attention. If you run a marathon slower than your 10-K time had predicted you should, give extra emphasis to your endurance.

Formulas such as this can help you set realistic goals, and then plan training and pacing accordingly. They can provide road maps for the unfamiliar territory of a distance you haven't raced before.

However, these numbers should not place artificial limits on performance or take the element of surprise out of racing results. Exploring the unknown and unknowable is a major reason to race, at any distance.

—The Evenly Paced Race—

Not everyone can run fast, but anyone can set and break personal records. The best way to break records is to ignore the runners in front of you and to concentrate on pacing your own race properly.

Arthur Lydiard, the influential coach from New Zealand, advises Pacers to "firmly resist the temptation to go with the local champion for the first half-mile." Lydiard says, "Only among top athletes who are fighting for championship honors should it be necessary to adopt this tactic. Among them, fast takeoffs in an attempt to break up the field are expected and warranted. But other runners are warned not to get tangled up in this sort of cutthroat running. They are the ones whose throat will be cut first." Lydiard doesn't advise starting slowly, but rather starting *cautiously*. He thinks the ideal starting pace "is one you know you can maintain all the way."

Every race is really two races. The parts are about equal in size, but they differ dramatically in content. The first half seems easy—often too easy. You know you should save something for later, but your body pleads, "Faster!" You find it hard to hold back. Then comes the second half, which is almost a different race. This is where you begin to hurt. You want to push on, but your body cries, "Slower!" You find it hard to hold on.

Bad races are the result of giving in to natural urges: running fast when you feel fresh and slowing down when you start to hurt. Good races are the result of resisting the instincts of freshness and pain: holding back when you feel best and pushing when you feel worst.

The first half of the race merely sets the stage. The last half is where the main performance takes place. This two-sided character of a race demands that the Pacer approach the event with a split personality. You treat the stage-setting half with the coolness and care of a technician. You do most of your planning for this part and run with restraint. In the second half, the race changes style, and you adopt a new role to match. Now you are an actor. You dispense with caution and inhibition, and run on creative emotion that can't be programmed.

Arthur Lydiard refers to even-paced running as "the best way to get the best out of yourself." You judge how even the pace is by again splitting the race in half. The closer the halves come to equal time, the more efficient the pacing has been. If you start faster than you finish, you lose considerably more speed in the last half than you gained in the first. However, you can also drop too far behind even pace in the early stages to make up the lost time later.

The safety range for pacing is about five seconds per mile either side of even pace. For instance, a 12:00 two-miler would want to run between 5:55 and 6:05 for each of the miles. These figures haven't been pulled from the sky. A review of world-record races indicates that most of the splits fall within one or two seconds per mile of even pace, and none of them varies by as much as five seconds.

If this pacing plan applies to the fastest and best-trained runners in the world, it also should apply to those of average ability. Perhaps attention to pacing is even more critical to the runner with less basic speed, less training background, and far less to gain from taking bold tactical risks.

Runners of all abilities can profit by timing at least the halfway split of races and later analyzing pace. You find the five-second tolerances by using this formula: subtract the fast half from the slow half, then divide the difference (in seconds) by the total distance (in miles). For example, if the halves of a 40-minute 10-K read 19:30 and 20:30, you slowed down by one minute en route—or about 10 seconds per mile. This slow-down factor was excessive.

Next time, for the sake of more economical pacing, start a little slower. You should be faster at the end, the only place where your time counts.

—The Cooperation on Race Day—

Running is a sport with few rules and many customs. This is a nice arrangement, because the sport needs few officials to enforce its minimal written regulations. Runners generally practice unwritten but customary honesty and courtesy, and we largely police ourselves.

These customs are the good manners of racing. They are the glue that holds together the alliance among three groups who make organized running possible: the participants, the promoters, and the people who share the places where we race.

Here is a refresher course in mannerly racing.

Fellow Racers

The basic advice: don't interfere with or intentionally disturb another runner's pace and concentration.

Start where you expect to finish. At a crowded starting line, choose a spot that matches where you'll be at the end. If you're an average runner, start in the middle of the pack; if fast, the front; if slow, the back. Don't force faster runners to climb over you to find running room, and don't handicap yourself by waiting for slower people to clear the line ahead of you.

Pass cleanly. Make sure you have room to go around without causing contact as you pass. Don't cross in front of the runner you pass until you're two or more strides ahead. If someone blocks your way and has room to move over, ask politely for the right of way.

Yield to the faster runner. When someone tries to pass you, give a fair fight ("fair" doesn't include the use of elbows or a zigzagging course as weapons). If you're being lapped on a track or a repeating course, move out to let the lapper through on the inside.

Finish what you start. Never begin a race planning to drop out along the way, or jump into the middle of one "for a workout." This confuses other runners who assume that you're going all the way and all-out, as they are.

Speak sparingly. You can, of course, give other runners a word or phrase of recognition and encouragement. But don't force them into conversation during the race, and never practice cheap psych-out tricks like telling someone how bad he or she looks. Concentration and confidence are easily broken.

Officials and Others

The key words here are: be tolerant of officials and patient with them. Managing a race is a big, thankless job, usually performed by volunteers and halfhearted recruits. Don't make their job harder than it already is, or they might not show up next time.

Pay or stay out of the way. Preferably, go through the approved entry process. But if you insist on running unofficially, don't spoil the race for runners who paid to be there. Don't get in their way at the start, don't take their drinks, and—above all—don't cross the finish line and mess up everyone's results.

Cooperate with the officials. Arrive and check in early. Get to the starting line on time. Get away from the crowded finish area as soon as you're finished running. Wait until all results are compiled before asking about your time and place. Thank the officials for their work. Better yet, volunteer to help at an upcoming race.

Remember, too, that we share the places where we run. Other people use them for other purposes. Nonrunners control access to these places and can take them away from us if we abuse our privileges.

Follow the rules of the road. If the racecourse is open to auto traffic, don't interfere with it (or risk your own life) by running in midroad, on the right side (the *wrong* one for a pedestrian), or repeatedly crossing the road to save steps. Stay in the lane reserved for the race.

For Mary Decker Slaney (United States), toughness has meant getting back up from her frequent mishaps — notably, the fall at the 1984 Olympics. Her surgical scars are outnumbered only by the records she has set and honors won.

Be friendly with the natives. Respect their property, and don't use it as a dressing area or toilet. Don't run these people down as they try to use the same paths as you do. Smile and wave if they say something nice to you.

Clean up after yourself. Hundreds of runners, each dropping as little as one race number or a postrace drink cup, can leave behind a lot of garbage. Don't drop yours.

—The 80-Percent Effort—

"Winning is easy," begins the actor in a television commercial. He's pretending to be ending a workout and has artificial sweat sprayed on his face and T-shirt. He slam-dunks a basketball into a garbage can, then tears off the wet shirt in one motion. "Give 110 percent, expect 110 percent—from everyone, everything."

He's selling deodorant, and at the same time promoting one of the worst sports myths. All you have to do to win, the ad implies, is to give more than your best.

Look more closely at those lines. They're both contradictory and illogical. Those terms "easy" and "110 percent" cancel each other out, and an effort beyond maximum is more than anyone can ever make. Yet the myth dies hard. Athletes think anything is possible if only they try harder. They run into more trouble from trying too hard than from doing too little.

Running demands that we ration our efforts and emotions over a long distance, not squander them all now and have nothing left for later. At any one time, then, we must intentionally do *less* than our best.

Trying to give "110 percent" in training invites destruction. Working too hard, too often is the major cause of injury. At special risk are runners who take too little recovery time after racing at or near total effort.

All-out work, challenging and exciting as it might be, tears us down. We repair that damage and prepare to accept more of it by staying well below the longest distance and fastest pace possible. The best building seems to be done at about three-quarters effort.

You probably accept this idea with your head, even if your heart and legs don't always get the message. Writers and speakers have been drumming it into you long enough with regard to training. What you'll find harder to believe is that you can also *race* better while putting out far less than "110-percent" effort. This can happen even with the fastest sprinters.

Lee Evans set a world 400-meter record at the 1968 Olympics that stood for 20 years. Tommie Smith and John Carlos won 200-meter medals at the same Games. All were coached by the late Bud Winter at San Jose State University. Winter preached relaxation. "The way to run faster is with a four-fifths effort," Winter taught his sprinters. "Just take it nice and easy. Going all-out is counterproductive."

He might have exaggerated by calling for 80-percent effort. He told athletes this to help them avoid trying to give "110 percent," and in the process tying themselves into physical and emotional knots. "The key," said this former instructor of World War II pilots who froze at the controls when they tried too hard, "is learning to relax under the pressure of combat. An athlete who wants to die for dear old Rutgers or San Jose State is as good as dead."

Athletes are more likely to succeed by relaxing and letting the trained-in ability flow out than by straining and struggling to exceed themselves. This explains why runners often say that their best races felt the easiest, or that they ran their fastest time when it was least expected.

A better word than relaxation might be "concentration." Being relaxed implies not caring, not trying hard enough. Concentrating means paying just enough attention to exactly what counts.

"Don't confuse concentration with consternation," warns sports psychologist Scott Pengelly. He says consternation arises from focusing too strongly on a goal and trying too hard to make wishes come true. Concentration means tuning into one's own body and mind signals at the moment, tuning out distractions, and letting what happens happen.

— The Limits of Planning —

You know Mark Nenow by his records. At this writing, no American has ever run a faster track 10,000 and no one in the world has run a faster road 10-K. You should also know the approach that led to those times. Mimicking Nenow won't give you the same results. But it may make you a more flexible runner, and I'm not talking about stretching exercises here.

While speaking at a running clinic soon after setting his world road record, Nenow seemed to have his role confused with that of most runners in his audience. The fun-runners in the crowd wanted advice on how to plot every step taken and analyze every move made. Mark, the serious athlete, talked of running with little planning.

He spoke without notes but had plenty to say. He answered questions with lots of "I don't knows," but his nonanswers contained much wisdom.

Nenow couldn't tell his weight and resting pulse, because he never checked them. He didn't want his blood tested or his muscles biopsied, because the results might have told him something he didn't want to know. He didn't use a computer to determine his training schedule, relying instead on instinct to tell him what to do.

He entered competition with only the most general of plans: "to stick my nose in it and run with the leaders as long as I can. That way, I either make a breakthrough or die like a dog."

He couldn't remember his times from recent races, which indicated that past performances didn't mean a great deal to him. He didn't say as much, but probably couldn't be bothered to keep those records in a diary.

Mark Nenow is a refreshing throwback to a bygone era of low-tech training. He certainly works hard, running well over 100 miles a week at a fast pace most weeks. You don't become a world-record-holder without doing that kind of work. But the way Nenow does it separates him from the majority of his contemporaries. He concerns himself only with the generalities of training steadily and racing hard, and lets the specifics take care of themselves. He *lets* things happen instead of trying to *make* them happen.

Such looseness requires great faith that the instincts guiding him are the proper ones. Nenow trusts himself to do the right things without help from a team of coaches and scientists, and without the backing of elaborate plans and logbooks.

His way doesn't always work. Instinct told him not to race between the world-record 10-K he set in April 1984 and the Olympic Trials that June. He thought he was getting too fit, too soon. Instead of making the U.S. team as expected, Mark placed 11th at the Trials. Then he immediately ran this country's fastest 5000- and 10,000-meter times of the year.

Such quick recoveries from disappointment are as much a part of Nenow's approach as his surprising breakthroughs. Failures are less devastating when expectations aren't excessive, and successes are all the more satisfying when they aren't planned.

Nenow says that all of his big improvements have come as "surprises." Because he doesn't set specific time goals, he sets no artificial limits on himself.

He once passed the midpoint of a 10,000-meter race faster than his 5000 personal record. More number-conscious runners might think, "Uh-oh, I can't keep going at this pace. Better slow down." Nenow kept going, willing to risk "dying like a dog." He didn't die but improved his 10,000 time by nearly a minute.

Mark may be short on knowledge of running theory and memory of his own practice, but he is long on wisdom. Anyone with a little know-how can complicate something simple, but only a wise person can simplify something complicated.

Mark Nenow's lesson to us all is not to let the planning and analyzing get in the way of the doing and enjoying.

—PART IV—
REPLAYING
THE RACE

CHAPTER 9

Reward Yourself and Rebuild Yourself

Toughness is judging success by your standards and recovering by your timetable.

—The Postrace Party—

John Steinbeck's *Travels with Charley* is less a travelogue on the country he toured than an essay on the nature of all trips. He writes, "My own journey started long before I left," and, "One goes not so much to see but to tell afterward." A race is like that. You draw the limits of racing success before the race starts—in the training you do before going to the starting line. Then you go through the race seeing little more than the finish line.

Steinbeck describes that sensation when he tells of his journey ending at the Continental Divide. There, he quit seeing anything but his home in faraway New York. "I was driving myself, pounding out the miles," he says. "The road became an endless stone ribbon, the hills obstructions, the trees green blurs, the people simply moving figures with heads but no faces." Steinbeck might have been describing a running event, because you race alone no matter how large the field. No one can share your work load, which becomes heavier the farther you go.

Racing is not much fun while you're doing it. The fun comes later when you talk about the experience. You race not so much to see but to tell afterward. The telling begins immediately, as you and a stranger hang onto each other in the chute and say, "Nice work!" The postrace rituals prohibit a runner from saying anything uncomplimentary to another.

You linger at the finish line, talking to anyone who will listen. You do some listening yourself to prolong the conversations.

Later you'll go home and tell the race story to your diary. It always listens patiently and never protests that you brag too much.

But first comes food. The rituals of racing must include a meal, preferably shared with other runners who have raced. The ritualistic prerace carbohydrate binge is a hollow occasion, because all you can talk about then is what you "might" or "hope to" do. That talk is always tinged with doubt. That last meal, taken in excess, can always return to haunt you on race day. A carbo-*reloading* party carries no such worries.

As you eat, you glance frequently at the watch on your wrist. There, frozen in digital time, are the minutes and seconds that you earned with your sweat. You indulge your pride for a full day after racing.

Zeroing your watch as you start the next run is the final—and perhaps most important—racing ritual. It says that no matter how good yesterday's race was, it's over. You can't live in the past. In this sport, you're only as good as your latest run.

Ron Clarke knew the feeling of setting world records more than a dozen times. He says that "invariably the exhilaration of achievement drains away." Clarke writes in his autobiography *The Unforgiving Minute*, "Perhaps the experience is not unlike that of a young man who has just celebrated his 21st birthday. He has looked forward to that occasion for so long. But after the excitement of the party, the congratulations and the gifts, he realizes that although now he is officially a man he doesn't feel any different. Life will go on much the same."

There are new races to run, new standards to meet and beat.

—The Damage Racing Does—

Racing is as destructive as it is exciting. Don't miss the excitement, but take special care in handling the destruction. Recover from the race as if it were an injury that takes time to heal. The healing period starts or stalls immediately after you finish, depending on how you treat yourself right away.

If you stop at the finish line and stay there, you recover slowly. The next few days' runs feel like they've been added onto the end of your race—or worse. But if you keep moving and cool down slowly, the damage done by the race is erased sooner. (See chapter 7 for further advice on cooling down.)

When you stop, the air cools instantly by what seems like 20 degrees. That's why you need to put on more clothes than you wore in the race. Change to a dry shirt even if the day is warm, jacket and pants if it's cool, and mittens and a cap if it's cold.

Resist the temptation to strip down next to naked and jump into a pool in warm weather, or to go right inside to a hot shower in cold weather. Either choice invites injury or illness later. Racing is enough of a shock to the body without subjecting it to such drastic temperature changes. Reserves to fight off illness already have been depleted by the racing effort. You don't need much of an extra jolt to trigger a cold or a case of flu.

You're Tough Enough If . . .

▲ *You massage the numbers to learn how much you've succeeded.*
▲ *You measure success by standards other than time and place.*
▲ *You view the race as its own reward, and awards as by-products.*
▲ *You record the event, in numbers and words, in your diary.*
▲ *You cool down as carefully after the race as you warmed up before.*
▲ *You carbohydrate-reload as much after racing as you loaded before.*
▲ *You respect the physical and emotional toll that the race took.*
▲ *You recover fully before trying to train hard or race again.*
▲ *You anticipate suffering a slight case of postrace letdown.*
▲ *You look forward to improving your times for seven or more years.*

Something else is guaranteed to happen if you don't keep moving. Your overworked muscles, saturated with fatigue products, stiffen quickly if you stop suddenly. They give you less trouble if you slow them by degrees.

Don't sit down immediately. Continue mild exercise in the form of walking, very easy running, or stretching—or some combination of these—for the next 15 minutes or so.

What you do on race day merely begins the healing process. Full recovery takes longer—much longer than you might imagine. Runners make the mistake of thinking they are well again once the muscle soreness disappears within a few days. Yet a much deeper and more subtle weariness lingers for many days after a 10-K race and many weeks after a marathon.

Racers (particularly those from the longest distances that have extended recovery periods) who jump back into full training and racing before the healing is complete keep sports doctors busy. The runner limps into the doctor's office a week after the race and complains, "I had no problem in the race, then this happened during yesterday's long run. What bad luck!" Luck had nothing to do with it. Heaping abuse on a battered body yielded this predictable result.

Racing is like a vaccine. The right dose can make you faster than you've ever been before, but too much of it can hurt. Racing too often without enough recovery and rebuilding time in between is the most common cause of runners' injuries.

Two innovative coaches from different sides of the world hinted at how often a person can or should race. Arthur Lydiard from New Zealand said that hard work should amount to no more than 10 percent of your total running. The late Dr. Ernst van Aaken of West Germany went even lower, limiting racing and race-effort training to 5 percent.

Using these ratios, you're limited to one racing mile or kilometer in every 10 or 20. One method of ensuring that races are spaced properly is to multiply the distance raced by 10 to 20, then not race again until you've put in that amount of easy running. This formula automatically lets you race more often at shorter, less-taxing distances, and less frequently at longer, tougher ones.

For Francie Larrieu Smith (right, from the United States), toughness has meant showing high-level durability. She competed in the first Olympic 1500 for women at age 19, as well as in the first Olympic women's 10,000 at 35.

An even simpler rule of thumb for clearing away the debris of racing is Jack Foster's now-familiar *one easy day for every mile raced*. If the world veterans' marathon record-holder needs that much, can you safely take less?

—The Meanings of Times—

You look up at the overhead clock as you cross the finish line. At the same moment, you click off the digital watch on your wrist. You compare the two times and accept the faster one.

When the race ends, you first want to know, "What was my time?" Later you need to know, "What does it mean?"

Distance and time are objective standards that can make winners of us all. The first victory is completing the distance. The second is running it faster than you have before or faster than expected this day.

Time for a distance tells more than simply what happened here and now. Unlike scores from most other sports, running results cross lines of space and years.

Nebraska's football score against Oklahoma on Saturday tells only what those two teams did against each other that day. It says little about how each might have done against Florida, or how this year's Nebraska team compares with one from 1970, or how well this team met its own standard of perfection. Running times transcend these limits. Ten-K runners from Nebraska can race against those from Oklahoma today and know how they might have done against those from Florida who raced someplace else.

Not only that, but people racing in 1990 can compete against records left behind in 1970. This year's runners can leave marks for people to break in the year 2000.

Best of all, you can compete against your own former self and win without beating anyone else. Time is your most important result.

Time not only lets you race this distance with these people. It also lets you compare your races with all other races at all distances you have ever or will ever run.

This is why you must know your time as soon as you finish and why you later work out its meanings. This time will be another page in your history.

You have your time. Now start processing it. Get it ready to go into your history book in a form you understand, and can compare accurately with earlier and later times.

1. *Compare the time with a known standard.* The race may have been an odd distance, like 7.6 miles. Your time of 52:36 doesn't tell you much, so you reduce it to a minutes-per-mile pace—6:55 in this case.

    Pace per mile carries more meaning than overall time because you can judge all training and racing by this same standard. You know immediately after making the per-mile calculations how much faster you raced than you normally run or how much farther you were able to hold a pace than you do in everyday runs.

2. *Compare the time with comparable races.* Times gain meaning as you run standard distances like 10-K, half-marathon, and marathon again and again—or as you race the same course repeatedly. You set personal records and store them in your diary and memory, to break or to know exactly how far you miss them.

3. *Compare the event with other events.* You might enter a 10-K race this week, a half-marathon next week, and an 8-K a few weeks later. So how do you judge the results from different distances?

Start by determining a normal slowdown/speedup factor from one distance to another (chapter 8 tells how). Create a more exact gauge for yourself by plotting your record per-mile paces for all race distances on graph paper. From this graph, you can see instantly if times are faster or slower than expected.

4. *Compare the first-half and last-half paces.* A dramatic slowdown in the latter stages indicates an overly aggressive start, probably to the detriment of your overall time. A closing rush much faster than the opening pace means that you probably lost more time early than you could make up late. (See chapter 8 for more pacing advice.)

5. *Compare projected and actual times.* A time considerably slower than predicted indicates that you have made pacing or training errors. Make corrections the next race.

On the other hand, a faster-than-expected time is cause for celebration. Not only did you do well in this race, but you can probably expect similar improvement across the board.

—The Years of Improvement—

Jack Foster, Priscilla Welch, and Carlos Lopes appeared to break the rules. They seemed to defy the normal effects of aging on runners. Past statistics had indicated that distance runners peaked in their late 20s and perhaps could hold that edge into their early 30s. But no previous results had suggested that a runner a decade older could remain competitive with the youngsters.

Foster, from New Zealand, was 33 when he turned from serious bicycling to serious running. He set a world record for 20 miles at age 39. At 41, he placed second at the 1974 Commonwealth Games with the fastest marathon of his life—2:11:19, which stood as the world's best time for masters for 16 years.

Welch, from Britain, was almost 35 when she started running. At 39, she made the British Olympic team as a marathoner. At 42, she ran her fastest time of 2:26:51 and won the New York City Marathon.

Lopes, from Portugal, won a World Cross-Country title and an Olympic 10,000 medal in his 20s. Then injuries almost ended his career. He came back in 1984 at age 37 to win the Olympic Marathon, then set a world record of 2:07:12 at 38.

Foster, Welch, and Lopes gave other runners their age hope that maybe they, too, could get fastest as they grew older. These three athletes didn't cancel out the natural advantages of younger runners all by themselves, but they did show that improvement was still possible after the theoretical peak had passed.

Lopes spent his late 20s and early 30s injured, and Foster and Welch weren't yet running then. They might have run even better at that age if conditions had allowed. As it was, the three proved that age isn't always as it appears on the calendar. Time spent running—the wear and tear of the years—may count for more.

A runner's legs can be old at 25 or young at 40. Jack Foster and Priscilla Welch still had young legs when they set their world masters' records.

Foster had been running about eight years when he ran his fastest marathon, and Welch about seven. Most runners apparently can expect to improve their race times for seven to 10 years.

Dr. Joan Ullyot, a physician and the author of *Women's Running,* thinks the improvement period averages about 10 years. One beauty of this period, she says, is that the clock can stop and then start later with no time penalty. Injuries stopped it for Carlos Lopes, who took almost 20 years to put in his best 10. The greater beauty of the 10-year clock, says Dr. Ullyot, is that it doesn't begin ticking until the runner begins competing. So a 50-year-old runner is promised the same span of progress as a 15-year-old.

Mike Tymn, a columnist for the magazines *Runner's World* and *National Masters News,* agrees with this theory but thinks a seven-year improvement cycle is more accurate. He notes that many types of natural cycles are seven years long. Marriages experience the notorious "seven-year itch." Gail Sheehy's best-selling book, *Passages,* identifies major life changes at seven-year intervals. Workers are advised to change jobs every seven years. Farmers worry about swarms of locusts devouring their crops every seven years.

You'll pass through cycles of your own. Welcome whatever surprising turns they might take. Each cycle represents an ending and a new beginning. When passing from one to the next, we give up something but replace it with something at least as good.

—The Story You Write—

The ultimate value of a diary (see chapter 4) is as a personal library of memories and dreams. You can open it to any old page and bring a race day back to life. You can call up that mental videotape and, from a few statistics on the page, re-create all you did and felt that day.

You can do this even easier if you've added words, sentences, and paragraphs to those pages. Make note of special people you met and experiences you had, of your dreams and plans, your hopes and fears, joys and frustrations.

Comment on your racing. This recording gives substance and permanence to ideas that otherwise would be as temporary as the moment, and to events that would immediately become as invisible as footprints left on the pavement.

You can be your own biographer. You don't have to be a talented writer to profit from a diary. You don't have to spend more than a few minutes a day writing in it.

Brian Maxwell wasn't trained formally as a writer. He was one of North America's leading marathoners in the 1970s, and later worked not as a journalist or an author but as a college track coach and a businessman. Early in his running career, Maxwell began writing stories about his races. Some of these found their way into print, but he would have written the same way even if no one had wanted to see the results.

Running has thousands of hidden Maxwells. Something about the activity, maybe the fact that we spend so much time looking inside our head, inspires the storyteller in us. We all love to talk out our adventures, and many of us take the next step by writing them down in diaries.

We now know that running is too good to belong strictly to the fast people. Writing is the same. It is too satisfying to be the exclusive property of professional writers. You may not have their talent. But they can't tell your story for you, just as no sub-four-minute miler or 2:10 marathoner can run your race for you.

Beginning to write is as simple as starting to run. Anyone who walks can run, and anyone who talks can write. But would-be writers face two mental barriers: the "I" phobia and the perfection syndrome. Don't be afraid to write "I" a half-dozen times per paragraph. The diary is your book, and modesty has no place in it. Here you exercise your ego, letting it run on at will. A writer who is free to talk about himself or herself should never be at a loss for words.

Writers only block up when they try to write too perfectly—when they put style before content, or when they feel the eyes of a critical audience looking over their shoulder. They work best by putting pen to paper and letting the stream of consciousness flow for an audience of one.

Let your observations and opinions rip. Don't worry about spelling, grammar, length, or organization. Adding, revising, and cutting come later, if ever.

Pour out your feelings to the diary. The numbers may be its brain, but the words are its heart.

—The Prizes You Win—

Two high school teammates walked away from a race they'd just run. One of them looked at the mass-produced certificate with a blank space where his name should have gone, wadded up the paper, and flung it into the weeds. "We work this hard," he said to his companion, "then all we get is this piece of shit."

Harried officials at the same race still were trying to sort out which 10 runners would receive silver bowls as their rewards. Many of those winners already had drifted away without bothering to collect their prizes.

A young runner stuck a Popsicle stick into an official's face. It read "97" to match the boy's finishing spot.

"What do I get for this?" he asked.

The official took out the frustration on the boy. "You've already gotten it," he snapped. "A race is its own reward."

The boy stared blankly. How could he be expected to know this at his age?

The same boy would stare in disbelief if he heard the story of Gar Williams, past president of the Road Runners Club of America. Williams used to win long-distance races regularly but always refused to accept his prizes. Instead, he passed them along to the next runner in line. "What a noble thing to do," you might think. The result of Gar's act was noble: giving a prize to someone who wanted and needed it more than he did. But his motive probably wasn't so much generosity as disinterest in this booty. He was sure enough of himself not to need this tangible reminder that "I'm special." His winnings from racing were less visible and more real.

One problem with awards is that they go to the wrong people. Runners who already have too many grab more each week. And runners who need these prizes to shore up their shaky motivation rarely take home more than a "finisher" T-shirt or certificate, or a "survivor" medal or ribbon.

More to the point, the place awards are too few. They go to a very small percentage of the field, and they wrongly imply that the only winners are the people who take home pieces of metal, wood, and plastic.

Fighting over these scarce items can sometimes bring out the worst in runners. It encourages complaining and conniving, trickery and deceit.

Runners who come away empty-handed may complain about the number and type of prizes. They may demand new award divisions to push more competitors aside on paper. Or they may literally shove competitors out of the way by resorting to tactical tricks. In extreme cases, runners may shortcut courses, take steroids, or doctor their blood to gain an artificial edge in the race for prizes.

Runners who struggle this desperately to win so they can earn tokens that say, "I'm special!" don't see that they already are special for having raced at all. They need to recognize that no one else could have run their race for them. Therefore, they are unique.

Your race itself should be rewarding. Setting a goal, training well, making an honest effort, displaying toughness and smartness, cooperating with other runners to improve yourself, recording a satisfying time—these are the true rewards of racing.

These rewards are available to everyone. But like all meaningful prizes, they must be earned.

—The Artist and the Hero—

One sad result of Jim Fixx's death is the impression left with the general public that he lived a lie and died in vain. Since July 1984, every runner has been challenged with the question, "If running is so good for you, why didn't it save Fixx?"

The best answer is that Jim didn't run primarily to save his life or to extend it, nor do most of us. He may have started running out of concern for his health. But he soon discovered, as all runners do, the more positive benefits that *kept* him training and led him into racing.

Fixx knew, as you do, that racing is less a physical act than a mental and emotional exercise. The physiological results of running are less immediate and dramatic than the psychological ones. Those could be found in other activities, even some sedentary ones, that provide the time to be creative and the chance to be heroic.

For Joyce Smith (Great Britain), toughness meant adapting to changing opportunities for women. She ran the 1972 Olympic 1500 when it was the longest women's race, and the marathon (at age 46) when it was introduced in 1984.

Creative

The "loneliness of the long-distance runner" is a myth that confuses being alone with being lonely. Runners look forward to the aloneness of a run.

Running gives you the chance to take charge of your own actions and thoughts. For up to an hour a day, you take full command of and responsibility for what you do and think.

This is your most productive hour. Not everyone needs to run, but everyone deserves an hour in every 24 to make something that is his or hers alone.

Much of life is now defined by what you *have*: job, house, address, degree, title, clothes, car. None of that counts when you run. You're stripped down to what you *are*: a body and a mind facing the elements of time, distance, and environment.

The pleasures you get from a run are both free and priceless. You can have them any day, but no amount of money can buy them. Only effort can.

The road and the runner's body are like a writer's paper and pen, a painter's canvas and brush, a sculptor's stone and chisel. They are common raw materials—nothing until the artist makes something of them. Anyone can pick up the materials, but only special care can transform them into art.

One definition of art is an uncommon thing made from common materials. An artist is one who brings order and beauty to the random, chaotic events of his or her life and who sees common things in uncommon ways.

By these definitions, runners are artists who find value in the simplest of acts and make the best pieces of art from the simplest of raw materials.

Heroic

Knowing how small you are helps you grow up, and running can always generate ways to reduce the size of your ego. No matter how many steps you have behind you, you're never more than one away from disaster. You learn in every bad run and every failed race that this sport can humble you.

Running also can make the most humble of us feel like a hero. Winning races isn't reserved for the person who finishes first overall or for those who place first in their divisions. Everyone who races can be a winner.

This sport, like all others, also carries the risk of losing. But this one, unlike many others, gives everyone an equal chance to win.

Its standards are both objective and personal. You don't have to measure yourself against other competitors, but only against distance and time. You don't have to beat anyone else to win, only your own records.

"I have found my hero, and I am it" has almost become a cliche in running. But it's still a rare idea in sports as a whole and rarer still in the outside world.

Most people still *have* a hero instead of being one. Most of them rank themselves, or let themselves be ranked, against everyone else doing what they do.

Most let themselves think in terms of what they *can't* do and not what they can. Most never let themselves be proud of themselves.

You need something you do yourself that makes you feel proud. Running as little as a mile farther or a minute faster than before can do that for you.

CHAPTER 10

Plan for the Long Run

*Toughness is mastering your biggest race of all:
the one with no finish line.*

— The Slowdown with Age —

Two facts on aging: (1) it may take another 10 years or so, but you'll slow down eventually, and (2) even if you're racing faster than 10 years ago, you're probably recovering slower.

Jack Foster, world masters record-holder in the marathon, offers guidelines for dealing with both types of slowdown. While he once competed equally with marathoners a decade younger, they always held the advantage in recovery. While he once averaged five-minute miles in a marathon, he couldn't hold that pace indefinitely.

Showing wisdom befitting age, Foster figured out sooner and better than most runners ever do how to back off after big efforts. His recovery formula became standard practice for smart runners of all ages. Even when he was racing hardest and training best, Jack took at least one easy day for every mile raced. He didn't stop running. But neither did he race again, or even train very long or fast, until the period of rebuilding had passed.

The second trick is harder to master. That is adjusting to life after the last personal record is set. The seven to 10 years, or whatever, of improvement will someday run out.

That time ran out for Jack Foster a long time ago. But he has adjusted well to life after PRs. Foster now races about a minute per mile slower than he did at his best. But he speaks philosophically about the slowdown. "The drop-off in racing performances with age manifests itself only on timekeepers' stopwatches," he says. "The running action, the breathing and other experiences of racing all feel the same. Only the watch shows otherwise."

Foster no longer compares his times, only his feelings. Times change, feelings don't. Everyone's time will eventually slow, but the effort and excitement of racing can remain constant throughout a runner's lifetime. If you don't look at the stopwatch, racing feels just like it always did. The anticipation and dread beforehand, the strength and strain during, the pride and relief afterward don't change—except that now you're revisiting old ground instead of blazing new trails.

You've entered a new cycle, a new stage in your evolution as a runner with new rewards to compensate for any lost speed. You've evolved into the third and final and highest stage.

You probably began running as exercise. Reclaiming basic fitness was the first goal, and going the first mile was both a struggle and an achievement. Sooner or later, though, you could easily meet Dr. Kenneth Cooper's exercise prescription of 12 to 15 miles a week, and you sought a new challenge. Racing beckoned. "Fitness is a stage you pass through on the way to becoming a racer," says another doctor/author, George Sheehan. The two stages have little in common. Exercisers run for health: racers seek performance.

But racing is also a stage passed through on the way to becoming a fun-runner. Performance eventually levels off, but the running life doesn't end there. The best of it is yet to come. In the final stage, the pressure is off. You may stay fitter than people who run just for fitness, and you may race better than people who run just to race. But those rewards become mere by-products. You no longer worry much about long-term health or short-term performance. The daily run itself has become its own reward.

—The Masters Who Last—

The ultimate winners in running are the masters, seniors, veterans—whatever you wish to call those who remain active into middle and old age. Winning is being able to run today and come back for more tomorrow. The biggest prize is wanting to continue with no finish line in sight.

You increase your prospects of lasting by minimizing foolish mistakes and needless suffering. You get hurt by running to extremes: too far, too fast, too often. You keep going by learning your limits and staying within them most of the time.

Lasting Tip One: Run Long Enough, but Not Too Long

Long enough to get most of the physical benefits isn't very long. Two to three miles may be the optimum length. After that, the returns diminish. You certainly can keep your body tuned with a few miles a day, a few days a week.

However, the body also has a head attached and the mind has different requirements. The early minutes of warming up and finding our rhythm aren't often pleasant. We wade through them to get to the good part that starts at about a half-hour. The first half-hour makes us fit. The second 30 make running worth doing.

You're Tough Enough If. . .

▲ *You unmask the three myths that make runners feel like losers.*
▲ *You learn that there can be gain without unrelenting pain.*
▲ *You learn that there can be more than one winner in a race.*
▲ *You learn that there can be running life long after your last PR.*
▲ *You accept your slowdown as inevitable and not really traumatic.*
▲ *You keep racing to renew old feelings, not to exceed old times.*
▲ *You view your career as a long race that must be paced properly.*
▲ *You last longer at racing by taking your races less seriously.*
▲ *You maintain a healthy skepticism regarding advice from experts.*
▲ *You keep asking tough questions of the experts and of yourself.*

At about an hour, the run quits being recreation and becomes hard work. Only the most serious of runners can afford to make the sport a second job by regularly putting in more than an hour, and few runners can tolerate hour upon hour of stress.

The perfect run falls into the 30- to 60-minute time range. This is long enough to be satisfying but short enough to remain hobbylike, long enough to make you want to come back for more but short enough to allow you to do so.

Lasting Tip Two: Run Slowly, but Not Too Slowly

Dr. George Sheehan, one of running's resident geniuses, says, "If the pace is too slow, it does very little good. On the other hand, a too-fast pace is self-defeating." "Comfortable" is the key word. Dr. Sheehan insists that the body knows, much more precisely than any watch or training schedule can tell it, what proper pace is.

If this advice sounds too vague, apply the one-minute rule of thumb: do most of the training at least a minute per mile slower than current race pace. Hal Higdon surveyed elite marathoners for a *Runner* magazine article on their training. He found that most of them did the bulk of their running a minute or so per mile slower than marathon pace.

For people who don't run marathons or merely endure them, 10-K race time provides a better guide. Compute the per-mile average of the most recent race at that distance, and add the minute or more to that pace.

Lasting Tip Three: Run Often, but Race Seldom

In oversimplified terms, training builds us up and racing tears us down. (This statement ignores the fact that some training runs can be harder than some races.) The secret of healthy running, then, is to build faster than you destroy.

The training runs, as defined in Tips One and Two, do the building. So do the occasional days of rest.

For Peter Snell (number 466, from New Zealand), toughness meant training like a marathoner for his track races. He laid the groundwork for his 1960 Olympic victory at 800 meters and his 800-1500 double in 1964 with 100-mile weeks.

Racing, including long and fast training runs taken at race effort, do the tearing. Treat them as a prescription item and take them only in small, measured doses.

Observe one of the "one" rules of race spacing: no more than one race a week, no more than one mile of racing in every 10 total, or at least one day of recovery for every mile raced.

Racing is as destructive as it is exciting. Don't forgo the excitement, but do carefully sweep away the damage.

—The Enjoyment Comes First—

People who decide that long-term enjoyment of running means more to them than short-term racing success must relearn their early lessons on pacing. However, this time the lessons don't apply to individual runs and races, but to the pace of their whole life as a runner.

Three runners tell of easing the pace that threatened their future as runners. Each found a slower lane so they could keep going longer.

Polly Peacock of St. Louis qualified for the Olympic Trials Marathon at 40. She then experienced a chain-reaction of injuries and finally came out of them with a new outlook. "Once you start doing well," she says, "there is a pressure to continue doing well. But once you stop running for a while, you wonder why you were putting so much pressure on yourself. I got out of the urgency to run 20 miles [in training]. It is such a pleasure to run four, six, or eight miles just for the fun of it." Peacock notes that "when my kids used to ask me to run with them, I looked for an excuse not to do so. Now I can run with them and enjoy it."

Roy Benson had been a runner for more than 30 years when he went to work full time with the Atlanta Track Club. Soon afterward, he gave up that job—in part, he says, because "I don't want my job to ruin my hobby. Running is my hobby, my first love, and I just don't want to burn out. I'm sure everybody thinks it would be fun to make a living out of running. But this work can be very demanding."

Dr. Walt Schafer teaches stress management at Chico State University in California and has written two books on the subject. Yet his professional and athletic interests once conflicted when he trained for races. He resolved that conflict. "After two or three years of overcoming the compulsion always to train hard, and the slight guilt of not doing so," says Dr. Schafer, "I now savor my running as never before. I am now entirely comfortable running an occasional race at a pace that I would have been slightly embarrassed about before." He began thinking of his training as "my daily minivacation. I depend on my 30- to 60-minute run for solitude, creativity, and energy." However, Schafer added that "I don't want to give up the exhilaration of sometimes running fast." He hasn't given up racing, but says, "I want to maintain a high level of fitness without the compulsion always to be preparing for the next race."

Jack Foster, the greatest over-40 marathoner in history, took this approach even at the height of his career. He says that he never thought of his daily running as "training."

"When asked about my training schedule," says Foster, "I always answered that I didn't train. I just went for a run each day." The New Zealander says that, to him, training meant bashing out highly structured workouts at maximum tolerable pace. He couldn't do that, *wouldn't* do that. "If that's what the coaches and physiologists say is required to be a champ," says Foster, "then I must remain a mug [average] runner."

In his peak years, Jack did plenty of running day by day. He couldn't have raced as well as he did without the hard work. But he says the fast racing came almost as a by-product of his outlook on running. He ran because he liked it, and by continuing to run he got very good at it—yet would have run this way even if it hadn't taken him as far as it did.

In Foster's view, "It has to be a pleasure to go for a run, looked forward to while I'm at work. Otherwise, no dice. This fact, that I'm not prepared to let running be anything but one of the pleasures of my life, may be the reason why I failed by just so much to win major races. However, this didn't bother me. Neither did the prospect of running 2:30 or even 2:50 marathons in the future."

—The Career-Long Outlook—

At the upper reaches of this sport, the One-Year Wonder prevails. Look quickly. The people you see leading this year's big-league races probably won't still be there next year.

The odds against climbing to the highest levels of running were always steep, and they're increasing. The stakes are higher than ever, and so are the effort and luck needed to collect them. Think how many runners this world holds. Millions. Then realize the infinitesimal percentage of them who ever reach, say, the top 10 in their event in any year. And for those few who get there, the stay at the top usually doesn't last long.

I followed the progress, or lack of it, of *Track & Field News*'s world-ranked athletes (10 per event) over a five-year period. Among the dozens of runners who gained at least one ranking, only three maintained a top-10 ranking for all five years. From year to year, slightly more than half the runners disappeared from the top 10—most of them never to return. Some 57 percent spent only one season on the list. Eighty-three percent stayed ranked for two seasons or less.

Of the many reasons for the relatively quick rises and fades of leading runners, the main one seems to be the effort required to reach the top. The harder a person works one year, the more difficult it is to repeat that work or work harder yet the next year.

It's a matter of pacing. Pace applies to matters beyond how fast you go in this race or that training run. It applies also to weeks and months, years and careers. The longer you want to run, the better job of pacing you must do.

For instance, think of your career one of two ways. It might be an ultramarathon where each year represents a mile. You cruise along at a nice, steady, comfortable pace, not letting any mile/year go so fast that it threatens the whole. Or you might think of your career as an endless interval workout. You run hard miles/years but only intermittently, taking time to recover between those efforts.

Racers, of whatever distance and ability, already fit the "interval" model. They alternately build themselves up and tear themselves down.

Pacing, then, aims to keep this destruction constructive. Those last two words aren't as contradictory as they sound. Mihaly Igloi, a Hungarian who coached many world record-holders before and after defecting to the U.S., used to say that training was like building a house. Each mile was a brick, and the total number of bricks—skillfully arranged—formed the structure. If everyday, submaximal runs are the building blocks of running, all-out races are the hammers that smash them. Runners who race are building to destroy.

Racing has its virtues and rewards. But stripped of its glamor, the race reduces to rubble some of what you've carefully erected in training.

How well you run between races determines the long-term strength and durability of the structure's foundation and walls. If they're well-constructed, a few broken pieces won't cause any serious harm so long as you take care to repair the damage right away before inflicting any more.

Before every race, check for obvious stress points and decide if they can withstand the demands of racing. During the race keep damage to a minimum. Afterward, take time to repair or replace the broken pieces, then add a few new ones to make the structure even stronger and more durable.

Constructive self-destruction means taking inspiration and motivation from the hard running that hurts, so you'll keep doing the easier running that helps. It means keeping a close watch on the number of races (and racelike workouts) in relation to the number of easier runs. It means spending more time building up than tearing down.

—The Gain After Pain—

You were introduced to the Great Lies of Running in chapter 2. One is, "There is but one winner in a race." Another is: "There is no gain without pain."

Pain equals gain? Training must feel bad if it is to do us any good? You don't start helping yourself to improve until you begin to hurt?

Before the running revolution of the mid-1970s, we swallowed these lines without placing question marks after them. Before we runners learned that running doesn't have to hurt all the time, before we saw the ultimate result of all that hurting, we were taught to glorify pain. We were coached to seek it every time we ran.

Derek Clayton, an Australian marathoner, served as a teacher in the pain-equals-gain school of thinking that dominated that earlier era of running when careers were brief. In the 1960s and early 1970s, Clayton trained hard—perhaps harder than anyone in his event ever has. When training to a peak, Derek ran up to 200 miles a week. He didn't just pitter-pat through those miles, either. He believed that any mile run much slower than race pace was wasted. So he averaged five-minute miles in training. A typical weekend run for Clayton would be a full marathon in 2:20 to 2:25. Not content with going that much slower than his sub-2:10 race speed, he would return

For Lasse Viren (number 301, from Finland), toughness meant knowing when and how to peak. He was beaten often between Olympics, but was unbeatable at the Games of 1972 and 1976 where he scored his double-double at 5000 and 10,000 meters.

that same afternoon for another 10 miles at five-minute pace. The reward for this routine was the world record he set in 1967 and reset two years later. The second mark stood for the next 12½ years.

But there was also a toll to pay. The immediate price was chronic fatigue. Clayton once tired himself so much that he smacked into a tree while training. The long-term price was chronic injuries. During his career Derek weathered nine surgical operations—from back to knee to Achilles tendon.

Sure, he reached some of the highest peaks in the sport. But he also descended into some of its deepest valleys. He left the sport thinking of himself as something of a failure for never having won an Olympic medal. Above all, he was a competitor and he never was at his best in his biggest competitions. To a competitor, a record only indicates that he has beaten a mechanical object—the clock. What he wants most is an Olympic gold medal, which signifies that he has beaten all fellow competitors. Clayton was injured during the 1968 Olympic Games at Mexico City, which he entered with the fastest time. He was hurt again at Munich four years later, when he also was the fastest runner in the field.

On retiring from competition before the Montreal Olympics, Clayton made this blunt, bitter, and revealing statement: "I can honestly admit now that I've never enjoyed a single minute of my running. I'm relieved to be finished with it." At his last finish line, all that pain hadn't equaled gain. Enduring all the pain of training, day after day, month after month, had simply worn down his soft tissues—along with his will to push on.

The pain had only added up to more and more pain. Finally, it had eroded his health and enthusiasm to the point where he saw no need to fight the pain any longer.

Clayton stopped, but not for good. His latest pains soon healed, and after a few months away from running he began to miss it. He didn't miss the 200-mile training weeks and the marathon races that had beaten him down so badly. He missed something about the daily routine of running itself.

Derek started to run again. Only this time, he limited himself to five or six miles a day—at a pace that would seem fast to anyone else but was comfortable to one with his talent. He seldom raced, and then only at short distances. Years later, Clayton still runs the same way. He says his whole outlook on running has changed: from being grinding work that he barely tolerated to being "one of the bright spots in my day."

He runs without pain. But who's to say he isn't gaining?

— The Life After Peaking —

There can be but one winner? Old-school coaches and modern media commentators encourage this thinking. They still promote the only-one-winner myth.

This implies that someone who wins on one level must then climb to the next higher one and succeed there. Ultimately, only the Olympic champion gets to stand above a mob of losers.

Jim Ryun did some impressive climbing when he was still a boy. But because he missed the very top by a single place, he has been unjustly labeled a "loser." At 17, Ryun made an Olympic team but was still too young to chase the gold medal—the only color that counts to one-winner thinkers. He would be a sure thing at the next Games, they thought. At 19, Jim set a world mile record. At 20, he broke it along with the 1500-meter mark. Then at 21, he "failed" at the 1968 Olympics.

He ran valiantly in Mexico City's thin air, losing in the 1500 only to altitude-trained Kip Keino. Ryun's critics showed no mercy. They said he had choked, had let his country down.

The next year, Jim psyched out so badly that he quit running. He'd violated the Satchel Paige Law. As long as the miler looked ahead to higher and higher peaks, he ran strongly, smoothly, confidently. He seemed to take little notice of who ran against him. Then he almost reached the top, stopped, and saw the hungry pack nipping at his heels. He did what Paige said an athlete should never do: looked back and saw that others were gaining on him.

This upset Ryun. He started running less to win than to keep from losing. He first lost his confidence, then his races. He dropped out of races to avoid the humiliation of finishing far back. Then he stopped completely, apparently for good.

After a year of no running at all, during which his weight jumped by 30 pounds, Ryun decided that he didn't want to end his career as a quitter. He hoisted himself back near the top, but the very peak still eluded him. At the 1972 Olympics in Munich, Jim was tripped in his heat of the 1500 and fell out of the race for the gold. The critics shook their heads smugly and again wrote "loser" beside the name Jim Ryun. For a time, the runner himself almost believed them.

When Ryun turned pro after Munich, he said, "I've never gotten anything from my running. It's time I finally started earning something for all this work." He might have been talking about not earning money before. But even "amateurs" were known to have cash slipped under tables to them in his day. Ryun probably meant that because he had never reached his most important goal—the Olympic gold medal—he had achieved nothing. If he couldn't be a famous Olympic champion, at least he could earn some money openly.

The pro track circuit never really took off. It folded after a couple of dull years, leaving Ryun without riches and with dwindling fame. But he isn't bitter about his fate. He, like marathoner Derek Clayton from the same era, rebuts the Third Great Lie of Running: "There is no life left for a runner after racing improvement ends."

Ryun, now in his 40s and half a lifetime removed from his world records, hasn't stopped running. He still races often, on the track and on the road, but seldom finishes first. "People beat me," he says. "But that doesn't trouble me, because I know that's a thrill for them. I feel that a person shouldn't be frustrated as an athlete or in life if they're giving their best and maybe don't come out on top."

Ryun wins no big races today, but who's to say he isn't a bigger winner than before? His race times quit improving more than two decades ago, but who's to say he isn't having the time of his life right now?

—The Fun-Run Era—

There was a time not long ago when only a few people ran well, and everyone else watched in awe. But then we became too busy running ourselves to envy even the Olympians for long.

We've known since the Running Boom began that this is too good a sport to belong exclusively to those who run best. Road races lavished fame and fortune on their winners, while welcoming large numbers of runners with less talent but serious commitment.

We now see that seriousness isn't even an entry requirement. An editorial in *Rocky Mountain Running News* notes, "Most racers today are loose and happy. Races have to be fun, fun, fun. Music, balloons, and colorful pennants abound. Many races encourage costumes or award prizes to the oldest, tallest, slowest, most patriotic, or best tandem. Race advertising tends to emphasize the frivolity rather than the competition of the event."

These events may not even be races in the traditional sense. Some look more like mobile parties, the place to go on a Sunday in lieu of a trip to an amusement park. Nowhere is this more true than at the largest U.S. event, Bay to Breakers. A survey taken after the San Francisco 12-K one year produced numbers that might shock the sport's purists: 38 percent of the entrants trained less than 10 miles a week; 12 percent ran the race without training at all; one in 11 wore a costume.

Nothing wrong with any of that. Bay to Breakers, Bloomsday in Spokane, and Peachtree in Atlanta—the country's three biggest races—are something-for-everyone events. They feature invited celebrities, anonymous but serious racers, people out for a good training run, and growing numbers of celebrants who wouldn't otherwise consider themselves "runners." The most serious runners, the least serious, and all degrees in between are welcome to find their own kinds of fun. These mass celebrations of running supply a healthy antidote to the "winning is the only thing" thinking that once dominated this sport and still prevails in most other sports.

However, the attitude shouldn't evolve into "winning is nothing." Competition in the traditional sense, a man and a woman beating all other men and women, has never been better. And the stakes, now expressed openly in dollar terms, have never been higher.

You might say you don't know or care who finishes first, but that misses the point. The people who race for the top prizes care very deeply and work very hard to get where they are.

You may ask, "Do the races really need these pros?" But that, too, misses the point. The pros need the races to hone and display their talents, and need us to make them look good.

You should be bothered by the new direction that road racing is taking only if the best of us and the rest of us can't continue to run together, only if the frivolous side of events overwhelms the serious side, only if the new trend toward fun-running turns this proud old sport into a joke.

For Grete Waitz (Norway), toughness meant pulling women's marathoning into its modern era. In three races spanning a two-year period (1978-80), she single-handedly dropped the world-best time from the mid-2:30s to the mid-2:20s.

—The Ultimate in Racing—

Beware of the "Guinness Syndrome." This is the attitude that the sport is worth prac-ticing only if it keeps producing record-breaking efforts.

Keeping records isn't the problem. Getting carried away in the pursuit of them is.

Chasing records can be normal and healthy. *Time* magazine essayist Frank Trippett writes, "It is easy to understand the performer's urge to do the improbable, the dif-ficult, the unique, the best. Claiming a record—any record—provides massage to the ego, varnish for the pride and a tick of celebrity." But Trippett adds that "society has become so proficient at keeping records as a way of celebrating the competitive trait, it is no wonder people get so carried away in the making and breaking of them."

No one is more proficient at record keeping than Norris McWhirter, a Briton who with his late twin Ross started the *Guinness Book of World Records*. No one gets more carried away than someone who tries to break into that book. Norris McWhirter says, "People crave delineation and points of reference. It's a matter of orientation, but it's also part of the natural competitiveness most of us have."

The Guinness people satisfy the human appetite to compete well, to stand apart from the crowd. We all crave this separateness to a degree, but in some runners the hunger can become overpowering.

Few of us are born with or ever develop the speed to separate ourselves from the pack at the shortest racing distances. But almost anyone can run longer. That's the story of the Running Boom: more people running longer. Before the Boom of the mid-1970s, being any kind of distance runner made you unique in your town.

Then came the great influx of runners-for-exercise, so you advertised your differences from them by racing 10 kilometers. The 10-K races grew crowded, so the marathon became the new home for the elite. Then the number of marathoners climbed until every office and neighborhood had one. Runners still looking to be different moved in one of two directions: to the ultramarathons or multisport triathlons, or to what Norris McWhirter calls "zanier outlets."

The zanies who couldn't run either fast enough or far enough to draw attention to themselves did it with bizarre variations on the running theme. We saw them run-ning races backward, or while jumping rope or balancing a bottle of champagne on a tray. We read of them dressing in tuxedoes, gorilla costumes, and bridal gowns. We even heard of nude racers.

No one would deny runners their right to have fun. But some antics crossed the lines from joy to a joke and from sport to entertainment. These performers ridiculed the athletes who ran seriously and well.

Pseudoathletes run as publicity stunts. True athletes run for the challenge and accept publicity as a by-product.

Ultramarathoners and triathletes are true athletes, looking to do what not just anyone would or could do. But their events, too, have grown up. The Western States 100-mile run and the Hawaii Ironman Triathlon now draw turnaway crowds. And this is not good news to athletes looking for uniqueness.

What next? Multiday races, runs across a state, and even a continent, double and triple Ironman triathlons?

The problem with these escalating distances doesn't so much concern the people who run them as those of us who don't. We may wonder, "Is this what I must aspire to? Is there something wrong with me if I don't or can't?"

We live in a time when there no longer are "good" and "bad" runners, only fast and slow ones. The revolution of the Running Boom years wiped away the inferiority complex of slower runners and let them be happy with whatever speed they could muster.

It's time for another revolution in our thinking. This one should let us take pride in whatever distance we can complete.

Tough Questions to Answer

"Any questions or comments?" I asked. We had come to my favorite part of any clinic, the two-way banter. Given the choice, this would be the *only* part of my talks. I'd rather converse than lecture anytime.

I don't invite feedback right away because people turn shy when they're part of an audience. The larger the crowd, the more hesitant its members are to shout out a problem or opinion. This audience almost filled the hall. So I gave a half-hour mono-logue, filled with rules of thumb on training and racing much like those in this book, before opening the discussion.

A man with the grizzled look of a longtime serious runner spoke first. "I've been waiting 10 years to meet you," he began.

I smiled and nodded—thinking, at last I've found a fan. The smile froze and slowly dissolved as he continued.

"I've been waiting all this time to tell you in person that I disagree with almost everything you've written in your books and articles, and said here tonight. I've broken all of your so-called rules, have never been injured, and am still improving after 20 years of racing."

The tough old runner gave a minilecture of his own, finally saying, "You've learned only what your own limits are, which is fine. Everyone should do that. But don't try to apply these rules to all of us."

After picking my chin up off the floor, I admitted that he had a point. At best, some of my advice only applies to some people some of the time. "I offer these general rules as starting points for further testing," I said, "so each runner won't have to waste an entire career reinventing the wheel. The least I hope to do is get listeners and readers to examine their own training and racing approach. Even if they reject every-thing I say, I've done them a small favor by making them clarify their own program and specify its points of departure from mine."

Later, I realized that I'd done my critic just such a favor. And he'd done me some favors in return.

At least he had *read* all those pieces, or he wouldn't have been able to disagree so specifically. And he'd come to this talk, if only to voice that disagreement. However, he mostly reminded me again that—despite having my name on the cover of books

For Priscilla Welch (Great Britain), toughness has meant beating women marathoners young enough to be her daughters. She began running at age 35, became an Olympian at 39, and won the overall New York City women's title at 42.

and at the top of articles—I didn't have all the answers for everyone. I still don't pretend to, and anyone who claims to know it all surely doesn't.

No runner speaks and acts with more certainty than one who has read a single how-to book or a half-dozen issues of the first running magazine he or she subscribes to. A little knowledge may be dangerous, but it also is comforting.

Only later, when a runner encounters conflicting information will he or she become confused. Confusion is a stage you pass through on the way to true knowledge.

The more you know, the more you see there is to know and the less certain you are of how much you really know. The more you practice the sport, the less accepting you are of "accepted" practices. You become a wise runner when you realize there are contradictions and exceptions to almost every running "rule." The more you read and hear, the less likely you are to believe what "experts" write and say.

The years on the road have let me in on many of running's secrets. Experience has taught me a lot, but has left me with full knowledge that I'll never have full knowledge of the sport.

Part of the enduring fascination with running is its continuing mystery. I hope this book has given you some answers, but I also hope that it has raised new questions that only you can answer.

—J.H.

─ APPENDIX ─

A Test of Toughness

In their testing at the Institute for the Study of Athletic Motivation, San Jose State University sports psychologists Bruce Ogilvie and Thomas Tutko (see chapter 1) isolated 11 personality traits that they consider to be the vital indicators of success in competition. Each of these factors can be measured by Ogilvie's and Tutko's 190-question Athletic Motivation Inventory. The psychologists define a mentally fit athlete as follows:

1. *Drive.* "Desires to win and be successful. Aspires to accomplish difficult tasks. Sets and maintains high goals. Responds positively to competition. Desires to attain athletic excellence."

2. *Aggressiveness.* "Believes one must be aggressive to win. Releases aggression easily. Enjoys confrontation and argument. Sometimes willing to use force to get own way."

3. *Determination.* "Willing to practice long and hard. Works on skills until exhausted. Often works out willingly alone. Persevering, even in the face of great difficulty. Patient and unrelenting in work habits."

4. *Guilt-Proneness.* "Accepts responsibility for own actions. Accepts blame and criticism even when not deserved. Tends to dwell on own mistakes and punish self for them. Willing to endure much physical and mental pain. Will perform even when injured."

5. *Leadership.* "Enjoys the role of leader and may assume it spontaneously. Believes others look to him or her as a leader. Attempts to influence or direct other people. Expresses opinions forcefully."

6. *Self-Confidence.* "Has unfaltering confidence in self and capacity to deal with things. Confident in own powers and abilities. Handles unexpected situations well. Makes decisions confidently. Speaks up for beliefs to coaches and other athletes."

7. *Emotional Control.* "Tends to be emotionally stable and realistic about athletics. Is not easily upset. Will rarely allow own feelings to show, and performance is not affected by them. Not easily depressed or frustrated by bad breaks, calls, or mistakes."

8. *Mental Toughness.* "Accepts strong criticism without feeling hurt. Does not become easily upset when losing or performing badly. Can bounce back quickly from adversity. Does not need excessive encouragement from a coach."

9. *Coachability.* "Respects coaches and the coaching process. Receptive to coaches' advice. Considers coaching important in becoming a good athlete. Accepts the leadership of the team captain. Cooperates with authorities."

10. *Conscientiousness.* "Likes to do things as correctly as possible. Tends to be exacting in character. Dominated by a sense of duty. Does not try to 'con' coaches or fellow

athletes. Will not attempt to bend rules and regulations to suit own needs. Places the good of the team above personal well-being."

11. *Trust.* "Accepts people at face value. Believes what coaches and teammates say, and does not look for ulterior motives being their words and actions. Free of jealous tendencies. Tends to get along well with teammates."

I took the AMI test in 1972. That was my 15th year of running competition, and I was still challenging personal records at the time.

The Ogilvie-Tutko computer matched my results against those from thousands of other athletes and ranked me on a 100-point scale. A ranking in the 90th percentile means that I would beat 89 runners in a 100-person race, while a score of 10 means that I would finish behind 90 of 100 runners.

My mental profile, from lowest to highest scores, along with comments from the test's creators, follows:

1. *Coachability* (below 5%). "Finds it extremely difficult to value coaching as a contributor to personal development. He will resent the demands placed upon him by his coach. This attitude may be reflected in his extreme independence, even to the point of being aloof."
2. *Aggressiveness* (5%). "Extremely nonaggressive athlete who rarely asserts himself even when pushed around. This athlete feels the aggressive elements of sports are unappealing and nonrewarding. For this reason, he will avoid situations where assertiveness is required."
3. *Mental Toughness* (15%). "Very sensitive, tender-minded athlete who rarely will face reality in a direct, positive manner. He expects someone to protect him from personal disappointment and is slow to readjust when it does occur."
4. *Self-Confidence* (15%). "Has almost no faith in his competence. He may show his lack of confidence by having a great deal of difficulty handling new or unexpected situations. It is rare for him to believe he could beat any opponent."
5. *Leadership* (15%). "Below average in his desire to be a leader. He will avoid positions of leadership and will not make decisions for others. He does not expect others to look to him for guidance or direction, and rarely will be forceful in his self-expression."
6. *Guilt-Proneness* (20%). "Not inclined to take personal blame when things go wrong. He does not consider physical or mental pain necessary in realizing his potential, and does not place value on conditioning. He may use minor injuries as an excuse, and they can negatively affect his performance."
7. *Drive* (30%). "Below average in ambition. He will set only modest goals for himself and will not readily accept challenges. He prefers to participate in contests where the outcome is reasonably predictable. Many of his feelings of competence come from areas outside of sports."
8. *Conscientiousness* (30%). "Below average. He is prone to break or bend rules which are contrary to his desires. He will interpret even just demands to be a denial of his individual freedom."
9. *Emotional Control* (45%). "Average. For the most part, he is able to handle his feelings. However, when competitive stress runs unusually high, tension may interfere with his performance. Since he has only capacity to handle bad breaks, they may diminish his self-control."
10. *Determination* (55%). "Average in sustaining effort to reach his goals. He will generally put in the required amount of training time, but probably will not devote much extra time. His persistence will fluctuate depending on his mood and the incentive involved."

11. Trust (85%). "Above-average. He accepts others without questioning their intentions. He can effectively communicate with other athletes and is not inclined to become jealous. Furthermore, this athlete also has a high tolerance for outside threats because of his trust."

Ogilvie and Tutko didn't use the word "wimp." Instead, they called me "tender-minded." I accept either term as accurate. I've never trained one of the 100-mile weeks that are standard practice for harder-working runners. I've never once collapsed from exhaustion as stronger-willed athletes do when they push themselves too far. But I've still done pretty well as a runner—once winning some state high school titles and a college scholarship, and later playing a small role in some of the nation's biggest events. I've raced at distances below 100 meters and beyond 100 kilometers. And though the speed and distance ceilings are much lower now, I still race at the current limits.

For Emil Zatopek (number 903, from Czechoslovakia), toughness meant breaking the old training rules. His training practices, unprecedented in their toughness, led in 1952 to the only 5000, 10,000, marathon-gold medal sweep in Olympic history.

ABOUT THE AUTHOR

Joe Henderson began running races in 1958 and published his first article on the sport two years later. He has since raced hundreds of times, and has written hundreds of articles on running as an editor with *Track & Field News*, *Running* magazine, *Runner's World*, and *Running Commentary*. This is his 14th book. Henderson now runs and writes from his home in Eugene, Oregon.